"I love Father Paul Jones. His writing, like the man, is deeply spiritual, refreshingly candid, and asks questions that open up new ways of seeing the gospel and the world around us."

—ADAM HAMILTON, Pastor; Author of *Creed: What Christians Believe and Why*

"Each day, Christians pray for the coming of the reign of God. Jesus taught us to pray, 'thy kingdom come on earth as it is in heaven.' Does God answer that prayer? Indeed, we have been given signs of what life is like under God's reign. In this captivating book, W. Paul Jones has taught us how we might taste the kingdom banquet before the feast is fully present. By living the church year, and living it deeply, we experience God's reign and know how it will be when the kingdom has fully come. As you read this book, this brilliant and gentle priest, who has a protestant mind and a catholic heart, will help you to experience the reality of that kingdom for which we pray. This book will nurture your soul, and help you to find islands of holiness in the sea of secularism in which we live."

—WILLIAM BOYD GROVE, Bishop (retired), United Methodist Church

REASONS FOR THE SEASONS

REASONS FOR THE SEASONS
Meditations for Living Meaningfully the Christian Year

W. PAUL JONES

CASCADE *Books* • Eugene, Oregon

REASONS FOR THE SEASONS
Meditations for Living Meaningfully the Christian Year

Copyright © 2016 W. Paul Jones. All rights reserved. Except for brief quotations in critical publications or reviews, no part of this book may be reproduced in any manner without prior written permission from the publisher. Write: Permissions, Wipf and Stock Publishers, 199 W. 8th Ave., Suite 3, Eugene, OR 97401.

Cascade Books
An Imprint of Wipf and Stock Publishers
199 W. 8th Ave., Suite 3
Eugene, OR 97401

www.wipfandstock.com

PAPERBACK ISBN: 978-1-4982-9212-2
HARDCOVER ISBN: 978-1-4982-9214-6
EBOOK ISBN: 978-1-4982-9213-9

Cataloguing-in-Publication data:

Names: Jones, W. Paul.

Title: Reasons for the seasons : meditations for living meaningfully the christian year / W. Paul Jones.

Description: Eugene, OR: Cascade Books, 2016.

Identifiers: ISBN 978-1-4982-9212-2 (paperback) | ISBN 978-1-4982-9214-6 (hardcover) | ISBN 978-1-4982-9213-9 (ebook)

Subjects: LSCH: 1. Church year. | 2. Title.

Classification: PR 4839 J15 2016 (print) | PR 4839 (ebook)

Manufactured in the USA   10/07/16

To
Cathleen Burnett, Rita Linhardt, Staci Pratt,
and the Board of Directors of
Missourians for Alternatives to the Death Penalty
who continue to teach me how

death-and-life form a primal rhythm

undergirding the reasons for the seasons.

CONTENTS

I. PROLOGUE TO THE CHURCH YEAR

A. Introduction | 1
B. Boredom and the Church Year | 2
C. Sacred Time, Things, and Space | 3
D. Big Celebrations and Little Hints | 6

II. LIVING THE SEASONS

1. Advent Busyness | 9
2. Advent Lens | 10
3. Advent Warm-Up | 12
4. Waiting, Always | 13
5. Advent Anticipation | 14
6. Advent Arrow | 16
7. Christmas Shopping—Yuck | 18
8. Half Empty, Half Full, and So What? | 20
9. Advent Conducting | 22
10. Advent Forgiveness | 24
11. Advent as Gracious Sterility | 26
12. Keys and the Masked Man | 27
13. Weary and Wearied | 29
14. O Come, O Come—Anyhow, Anyway! | 31
15. Christmas Eve Trust | 33
16. Not Christmas Day at All | 34
17. Christmas at Dawn | 35
18. Christmas as Deadly | 36
19. Christmas Past | 37
20. Christmas Present | 39

CONTENTS

21. Christmas Future | 41
22. Christmas—a Bad Idea? | 42
23. Christmas Love Affair | 44
24. Christmas as Always | 45
25. Christmas as Big Enough to Be Small | 46
26. Ironies of Christmas | 49
27. Tenses of Christmas | 50
28. Final Christmas with Thanks | 52
29. New Year's, Jesus, and the Call | 55
30. Epiphany Wisdom | 57
31. Baptism—His and Ours | 58
32. Candlemas by Candlelight | 59
33. Meeting Jesus Again and Again for the First Time | 60
34. Lost and Found | 61
35. Mardi Gras as a Bookend | 63
36. Ash Wednesday as a Walden Pond | 65
37. Ash Wednesday as Compline | 66
38. Lenten Choices | 67
39. Societal Rewards as Christian Sin | 69
40. The Wall, Lent, and Passing the Peace | 71
41. Lenten Discipline as Joy | 73
42. Positively Negative and Negatively Positive | 74
43. Lenten Forgetting through Remembrance | 76
44. Lenten Inventory | 78
45. Lent as a Both/And | 80
46. Lent and the Power of Words | 81
47. Palm Sunday and the Last Chapter | 83
48. Uncertainty and Happy Endings | 85
49. Fortunate Betrayal | 88
50. Last Supper That is Not Last | 90
51. Foot Washing—Dirty or Not | 91
52. Good Friday and the Defining Three Moments | 93
53. Good Friday and the Way of the Cross | 95
54. Good Friday—Funerals and Beyond | 96
55. A Hellish God | 98
56. Hell and Holy Saturday | 99
57. Holy Saturday and the "Sure Thing" | 100
58. Marshmallow Easter | 101

CONTENTS

59. The Eyes Have It | 103
60. Dum de Dum Dum | 105
61. Easter Stories | 106
62. The Tomb as Cave | 108
63. Easter Savoring | 110
64. The Joy Called Easter | 111
65. Easter Peace | 113
66. Easter Fear | 114
67. Resurrection of the Small | 115
68. What's in a Name? | 117
69. Killers at Easter | 118
70. Mother's Day and the Day After | 119
71. Sucker-Stick Ascension | 121
72. Pentecost and Intertwining Liturgy | 123
73. Pentecost and Ascension Fear | 124
74. Persistent Flame—A Second Thought | 125
75. Pentecost as Easter | 126
76. Pentecost Diversity | 128
77. Trinity: Three as One or One as Three? | 129
78. Valentine Jesus | 131
79. Marching with Jesus | 132
80. Memorial Day as Once It Was | 133
81. Memorial Day and Cemetery Remembrance | 134
82. Father's Day and Good Old Dad | 135
83. Independence Day and Christian Patriotism | 136
84. Independence Day for All | 138
85. Transfiguration as Promise | 140
86. Labor Day and Beyond | 140
87. Halloween or the Goblins Will Get You | 142
88. All Saints', Souls', and Imaginative Memory | 143
89. All Saints' and Loneliness | 145
90. All Souls' Day and Going Home | 146
91. Christ the King—Maybe and Almost | 147
92. Is This Mess God's Idea? | 148

I. PROLOGUE TO THE CHURCH YEAR

A. INTRODUCTION

TIME IS WHAT WE walk through—and it is that which walks through us. Even if we are unaware, it snatches away parts of us as it pushes us relentlessly toward apparent oblivion. Thus unless we become gifted by the ability to discern time as having a meaningful pattern, living begins to feel like the unwinding of a kiteless ball of string. Unless time is textured with the joys and pensiveness of highs and lows, existence is a frivolous game. Unless time gains momentum in luring us forward by promise, we get drained— as one tedious day drags out the next, fatigued into a nameless sameness. Unless our days and weeks and months and remaining years have more than trivialities to distinguish them, we are swallowed up in a faceless blob.

Priceless, then, is the endowment offered every mindful Christian— that of having time redeemed. Christianity wraps us in a mysterious patterning of beginnings impulsed toward enriched ends. Spiritual seasons enfold the physical turnings of our beloved earth, as the remembrance of things past give spice to the evolving whole. Christianity choreographs time into dance, inviting us to sway with sacred rhythms—of the ordinary and extraordinary, of intensity and leisure, of togetherness and solitude—as the multicolored threads of our own living are woven into the expanding tapestry of God's becoming.

Reasons for the Seasons is a book composed of ninety-one meditations offered as resources for personal, family, and group use in experiencing and pondering more deeply this Christian movement of time. They have emerged over many years of my own pilgrimage—as a United Methodist pastor, a university and a seminary professor of theology, a Trappist Family brother, a Catholic priest, and now as resident director of the Hermitage

Spiritual Retreat Center on the shores of Lake Pomme de Terre in the Ozark hills of south central Missouri—where restorative solitude and social passion creatively interact through these rhythms of the church year.

B. BOREDOM AND THE CHURCH YEAR

Although I am not sure I have ever experienced pure boredom, it seems to be a disease afflicting many persons today. Apparently it is the absence of feeling much of anything about anything. It must be sad to have little more to look forward to than television's *Jeopardy* or *Wheel of Fortune*. How monotonous for life to be a clothesline of tattletale grey days slung between the Super Bowl and the World Series. "Much ado about nothing" is Shakespeare's name for it, and Ecclesiastes provides the Scripture: "All things are full of weariness . . . there is nothing new under the sun" (Eccl 1:8–9 RSV).

The church has continuously skirmished against such boredom, above all by providing the church year as a creative alternative to the secular calendar. The intent is to fill our days and months with a rhythm of highs and lows, ins and outs, ups and downs—weaving a multitude of emotions into a marvelous adventure. The overall structure of Christian time is the triadic cadence of *promise, gift,* and *response*. Twice a year this triad is rehearsed with self-conscious intensity, serving us like a "boot camp" in which the requisite behavior is so practiced that it becomes second nature—for living meaningfully the "Ordinary Time" between these rehearsals. These triadic seasons function a bit like periods of disciplined scale practicing so that Beethoven might flow naturally from our fingers without need to take thought.

This rhythm of the church year begins in early winter, with the first of the two cycles being the season of Advent [*promise*], Christmas [*gift*], and Epiphany [*response*]. This is followed by the first of two segments of "Ordinary Time" into which these rhythms are translated into daily living. The second rehearsal cycle begins in the spring with Ash Wednesday—as Lent [*promise*] Easter [*gift*] and Pentecost [*response*]. The second segment of "Ordinary Time" follows, itself climaxing the whole church year as *fulfillment* in the final Sunday feast of Christ the King. In this climax we experience as foretaste how the yearly cycles participate together in a spiral—as all of history is mysteriously being drawn in its own ongoing rhythm of *promise, gift,* and *response* into the kingdom of God. Thus although the next Sunday begins the church year anew with Advent, this is not to be

I. PROLOGUE TO THE CHURCH YEAR

understood as a repetition as much as a spiraling ever closer to completion—as individually and as a whole we are passing into the God who is becoming "all in all." Each year's revolution participates in a continuing cycle of passing into eternity.

Each triad begins with a time of aching, of yearning, of craving for more—in effect, for fulfillment. We are lured into receiving as answer the gift that only God can give. This reception, in turn, evokes as response a missional call into action. Thus Advent's longing, through the incarnational gifting of Christmas, lures us into Epiphany as a call with the Wise Ones to live the light of the good news into the farthest corners of the earth. Then, after a period of application, the Lenten craving for forgiveness through the Easter resurrection as reconciliation gifts us into a newness of life that empowers us into Pentecostal mission on behalf of the poor, the needy, and the rejected everywhere.

These two intense triads as "dress rehearsals" train us by participation in these extraordinary rhythms so that we begin living them instinctively in the daily patterning of the sixteen or so weeks of "Ordinary Time" that follow each triad. Additional seasonings are sprinkled along our adventure in the form of remembrances—saints and past events in order to counter our forgetting. There are cultural occasions as well that provide a final spice, such as Mother's Day, our three summer holidays, Thanksgiving, and Halloween, all capable of being baptized into deeper meanings.

Thanks to such rehearsals, the sunrises of our "ordinary" days can be colored with hints of resurrection; daily work can be etched with a sense of Pentecostal calling; disappointments can be mellowed into Good Friday companionship; coffee with a friend can foreshadow the depth of a shared chalice; and as an evening finale we can offer our days as a thankful ascensions into God—even if some days feel like only a prodigal report from "a far country." With time transformed into such an adventure, how can life be boring?

C. SACRED TIME, THINGS, AND SPACE

All of us are creatures of habit, every one. We sit in the same pew each Sunday, drive the same route to work, start the grocery cart down the same aisle, and peel an orange in our own favorite way. Such sameness can give life a sense of security, for deep in us is the longing for life to have an ordered meaning. Some of us had mothers who sang the ditty and "religiously" followed it, the one about Monday being washday, Tuesday ironing, all the way to a Saturday night bath as our weekly "vespers" in preparation for Sabbath freshness. No matter what our particular ordering, when it is interrupted, we feel disoriented.

Such ritualizing applies not only to our time, but also to the prioritizing of things. We have favorite foods, colors, songs, and people. Without such ordering, life would become overwhelming, forcing us each morning to re-sort things into an order sufficient to re-identify who we are, where we are, and what we are to be and do. While this need for order is universal, the difference that makes all the difference is the *motive* that impulses our ordering. What a profound difference it makes if our patterning is done in order to satisfy the expectations of others. Or if it is the result of coveting, in which the design is to thrust one's self into the center of whatever is going on. Or if it reflects the longing to find one's self by losing our self in something greater. To be a Christian entails the latter—with our personal ritualizing being transformed by being taken up into an embracing divine ritual.

As appealing as all this may sound, there are constant distractions in modern society that threaten to diffuse our efforts as Christians to live intentionally in this manner. In this regard, monks have an advantage, for their geographic isolation permits them to restructure their environment so as to incarnate more explicitly this Christian dynamic. Thus they largely replace the secular calendar, shaping the anatomy of their seasons with the sacred rhythms of the church year. In fact, each day is bequeathed its own distinctive flavor—whether it be the eager anticipation of Christmas Eve midnight mass, the intense drama of Easter Vigil, or just the tease of being Monday in the fourth week of Lent. How different all this is from a society whose counting is of shopping days until Christmas. Thus the season of Advent for monks takes on something of the atmosphere that many of us experienced as children, bathing the accoutrements of things and space with a childlike aura of promissorial anticipation. From there the seasons move on with a lilt, trimmed the color of highs and lows, spiraling us as participants into a finale. This holistic rhythm is echoed in a matching pilgrimage structuring each day. The monastery takes seriously Jesus' injunction to live only in the "now," with God dealing out time only one day at a time. Each morning begins with a full cup to be drunk to the last drop, and returned empty each evening, never knowing if that day may have been the final sip of the last drop of our life. And if there is a

I. PROLOGUE TO THE CHURCH YEAR

next day in being awakened in the dark hours for Vigils, it follows that at dawn, Lauds ("praise") is our thanksgiving for a priceless gift—of an utterly unique day of life, being for us a mini-Easter resurrection from a deathlike sleep. Indeed, "Christ has risen, Alleluia!"

With life so blessed, each meal can be celebrated as a mini-Eucharistic act of gratitude. Work can begin with a mini-Pentecostal prayer for an empowered sense of calling. Evening Vespers can be our Christmas gift to God in lifting up our day with interest. And Compline ("complete") can be our nightly finale as a mini-Good Friday of dying with Christ into the Great Silence, "Into your hands, O Lord, I commend my spirit." Yearning, promise, foretaste, gift, thankfulness, hope—these are the favorite herbs in the menagerie of Christian seasonings. Bells serve as delightful contrivances to awaken such mindfulness, enriching the commonplace with an uncommon choreography. Colors receive their liturgical due—expectant raspberry, joyful yellow, innocent white, spring leaf green, iris purple, firelit red. One can even tell the seasons by the aromas.

At its deepest level, Christian living is an exquisite intertwining of Christmas with Easter—a jubilant "yes" sung to the length and depth and height of creation. "In him it is always 'Yes'" (2 Cor 1:19 RSV) The soaring of a hawk, the softness of an adopted kitten, the aroma of freshly baked bread, the later piano concerti of Mozart, an elder person's peace in sensing her end, the mocking bird's definitive vesper proposal regarding the existence of God. With every sense attuned to the glory of God, we taste and see that the Lord is good—for many are the hints eliciting our duet with God: "Behold, it is very good" (Gen 1:31 RSV).

Because our postmodern society is so persistently inhospitable to faithful remembrance, discipline is essential for the Christian. Without rehearsal of the church's rhythms for time, place, and things, our senses become dulled, our motives become subverted, and our actions are rendered routine. This is why Christian oases are deeply needed—spaces with resourcing for dancing this alternative cadence as though no one is watching—warding off a secularism that is determined to paint us with the motivations of competition, individualism, materialism, and status. In contrast are days of conformity in controlled cubicles without windows, lunch breaks pummeled by advertising on every surface, evenings numbed by television impulsed by the icon of commerce—these are the instruments that can relentlessly dilute us Christians until unknowingly we find ourselves living as functional atheists. Atheism resulting from a reasoned decision is actually rare, but increasingly widespread is an atheism of dulled attitude carved out by the daily erosion of modernity. For our suffocating souls there may be no better medication than the sound of monastic chanting coaxing the evening to sleep, walking out into a canopy of stars that stretch at least forever.

The church is sometimes disparaged for appearing to be isolated from the marketplace, for being out of the mainstream, for being a dusty remembrance of times past, for being a refuge for those who don't seem to fit in. Perhaps. But perhaps again the church may actually be a fledgling remnant before its time, modeling a richly patterned living that keeps lively for the future the hope that neither the Milky Way at night nor the chanting birds at dawn sparkle or sing in vain.

D. BIG CELEBRATIONS AND LITTLE HINTS

Christianity's central celebrations, then, such as Christmas, Easter, and Pentecost, are corner supports for the church's sweeping *wholesale* canopy on which are fastened the lanterns of our *retail* living. Together they shape and nurture the apertures of our savoring and the prisms for our seeing. Christmas, for example, as our celebration of God's decisive gift in providing a center point for history, divides time into "before" and "after"—exposing as unique the moving point called "now." Each moment, each hour, each day, each year—these are Christmas gifts in being unlike any other intersections that have ever been or will ever be. Living intentionally each "present" is to participate in the giving and receiving of "presents." In being made aware, there is joy even in the lilting cadence of crackling breakfast cereal, the waving to fellow drivers on the freeway, surprising others with an elevator smile, calling an acquaintance spontaneously, complimenting a weary co-worker, recognizing as "vespers" one's turning into a driveway that promises hugs at the door. These are the gift-wrapped hints made recognizable when Christmas becomes an intentional rehearsal into Christian mindfulness.

So it is with Easter, as the resurrection extended as hope to the whole human race becomes a marinade flavoring each day. With Easter eyes, dawn becomes a pledge that darkness will not have the last word; evenings bring remembrance of how ordinary expressions such as "Thank you," "I'm sorry," and "I appreciate you" have resurrecting power. Likewise Pentecost, as the Holy Spirit's birthday gift of the church as leaven for the world,

I. PROLOGUE TO THE CHURCH YEAR

provides training for recognizing Christ's daily disguises in the faces of the hungry, sick, neglected, and imprisoned. Thus Christian living results by decoding the big celebrations into hints and guesses about the little things, thereby incarnating, resurrecting, and empowering the ordinary into the extraordinary.

This may be why All Souls' Day has special significance for me. Death is the deconstruction of all the big things, and without awareness of its leering face, we become blinded to even the little things. Hearses do not pull U-Hauls. T. S. Eliot calls death the "primitive terror," haunting all of life as a relentless cannibal. All Souls' Day is the church's dramatic defiance of death. In Mexico, Christians call it the "Day of the Dead." Each home has a tiny altar on which is placed a round bread as symbol of eternity, a candle as the light of Christ, and marigolds as a flowered aroma for the dead. The celebration is rendered personal with photos, mementoes, and a favorite food of the beloved, placed in a new dish. Incense guides both families and spirits to the cemetery where graves are adorned with flower petals in colorful designs. A priest blesses each grave, and while a band plays, relatives with friends picnic among the so-called dead—often frolicking with them by candlelight until midnight.

Monks, too, are adamant about defying death. At daybreak on All Souls', we enter the cemetery to bless each grave with the water of baptismal promise and the rising incense of hope. Then we tell stories that enflesh each deceased person, "waiting" there in rest. It is indicative that our tales are rarely about "big" things, such as honors or major accomplishments. The resurrecting worth the telling engages us with the little things, rebaptized with knowing smiles or laughter. This past year, our monastic "defiance" involved cherishing Br. Chris's dexterity in playing "Little Brown Jug" with concurrent harmonica and guitar. Fr. George's remembrance was his legendary pea soup. Fond smiles recalled Fr. Donald's adornment of our Christmas trees with strung milk caps. Fr. Richard's acclaim was that patient smile as a brain tumor squeezed his mind into oblivion. As for Br. Dominic, we ventured that he was probably wearing his ubiquitous red cap even in eternity.

Graves tend to bury the "big things" over which much of our living was consumed in fretting; instead, time winnows our perspective into resurrecting the little things that are precious in God's eyes. Out of the many words Jesus spoke to Peter, he needed to remember only three: "Feed my sheep." A child's voice heard over a fence was all that Augustine needed never to forget. What mattered in Francis's life was the morning he wandered into a church where the reading "happened" to be about giving away everything to the poor. A "big little" that occurred to me was the day my first grade teacher appreciated my purple improvisations outside the lines.

This is why the church offers us the big days as exercises in recognizing the small—the "in as muches." (E.g., Matt 25:40 KJV.) So equipped with opera glasses, as if were, the curtain opens on our earth as the theatre of God's glory. "Be renewed," Paul exclaims to us, "in the spirit of your minds" (Eph 4:23 RSV). And to the lukewarm local church, John echoes God's counsel: receive my "salve to anoint your eyes, that you may see" (Rev 3:18 RSV).

II. LIVING THE SEASONS

1. ADVENT BUSYNESS

Busyness has a naughty way of attacking our Decembers, so much so that only for children does Christmas not come quickly enough. No matter how far in advance of Thanksgiving the stores urge us to do our Christmas shopping, Advent is a rush and Christmas an exhaustion. Even the church seems to hustle us along at an unwelcomed pace. As we observed, the first Sunday of Advent comes only one week after celebrating Christ the King as a climaxing of both the year and of history. Surely we deserve at least a few weeks to bask in that Divine crescendo, to let the finale of Handel's *Messiah* echo deliciously in our souls—that "He shall reign for ever and ever. Amen."

Probably that is unrealistic, for it doesn't take long after that final church "high" for things to return pretty much as they were before. The Chiefs lost another game, the kids' yelling is off key, and the phone regains its annoying persistence. From all appearances, Christ the King hasn't come after all, and here we are, one week later, starting the yearly cycle over again—with Advent yearning once more resurfacing.

It sometimes seems that this is the way things go, round and round. Metal rusts, wood rots, plastic cracks—we all die, and the circle starts all over again without us. For those of us who are now looking back up the slippery slope from the perspective of aging, life can seem like an elongated preparation for hospice care.

Thankfully the church understands, intensely aware of the pathos of life lived without hope. That is why Scripture itself ends in a final hope: "Come Lord Jesus." This is why Advent re-begins with our singing "O Come, O Come Emmanuel." "Come" is the overarching Christian word that bathes all our seasons and days with an Advent aftertaste. Without a "yet to be," "that which was" pollutes the present as only "more of the same."

The "come" that characterizes our Advent hope is actually triune. First, we celebrate the God who *came* as a child, so that the child within us, as with Elizabeth, can leap with playful joy at the thought of our divine familial adoption. Second, Advent is a yearning for the One who in coming promises to *come again*. Picasso was right in declaring that "it takes a long time to become young." Our Advent faith knows a shortcut. Christmas is the gift of dreaming with Don Quixote the impossible dream—of when justice and peace shall embrace with a kiss, when the gentle manger calf will romp with the lion, and when Jesus proposes Mickey Mouse for modeling our second-childhood as he leads the Epiphany parade.

The third Advent "come" may be the most important promise of all. The One who came, and the One who will come, *comes now*, ongoingly, in each moment. The past and future tenses intersect as an ever incarnate "present." Christ is Emmanuel, "God with us." The One who "was" and ever "shall" be is the One who "is" *now*. What hurts most about life's hardships, sufferings, and disappointments is the feeling that we are enduring them all alone. Advent is our exercise in learning to know better. Martha was right when she identified Jesus as the one "who is coming into the world"—continually as a companion presence (John 11:27 RSV).

Thus the Advent Christian exists in three time zones, lived simultaneously. Past yearnings and promised futures gain their substance by converging as Advent foretastes. The "came," the "will come," and the "coming," together are fulfilling Christ's incarnational promise that "where I am, you may be also" (John 14:3 RSV). Life is an advent journey lighted by Christ's assurance that "we're in it together, every step of the way."

2. ADVENT LENS

As if it is not difficult enough, as we noted, to have only one week between ending the church year and beginning it all over again, the lectionary readings for this intervening week warrant an R rating. Seemingly they were chosen to provoke nightmares. Zephaniah, Daniel, and Revelation appropriately deal with a God who is coming, but their portraits of this coming are downright ominous and their words startling—"terrify," "anguish," "devour," "crush," "trample," "fall," and "burn." If the Advent yearning is supposed to be for one returning like that, count me out! I'm out of here.

Yet, ironically, as we do enter this first week of Advent, the scriptural mood changes, drastically so. By Wednesday the themes of judgment,

II. LIVING THE SEASONS

punishment, and rejection have become replaced by imagery of "feeding." Isaiah portrays God's coming as bringing a banquet for all, when the veil disconnecting persons will be removed as an invitation for universal embrace. Death shall be destroyed, the prophet insists, tears shall be wiped away, and the world will be healed. Responsorial Psalm 23 escalates this theme by word-painting God as a shepherd, one who is not the cause of life's glass-strewn back alleys but the one who walks with us even through "the valley of the shadow of death." More mesmerizing still is that the banquet promised for the end of the Advent pilgrimage is being "prepared before *me*" now, before each of us, with the Eucharist as its foretaste. The crescendo in Matthew's portrait is of people flooding from every direction, placing at Jesus' feet the crippled, deformed, blind, and mute—and he cures them all. This is the heart of the Advent promise!

What, then, are we to do with those ominous pre-Advent readings? We are sometimes warned against being "cafeteria Christians," picking and choosing among the Scriptures. But that is what all of us do, for inevitably we have no option but to look at Scripture through some particular lens. And the one chosen will draw certain things into the foreground while others recede into the background. As to which lens is best, which is most faithful, this is a fundamental wager that each of us must make. For me, these early Advent Scriptures provide the best lens for viewing *all* of Scripture. Since for Christians Jesus is the definitive personification of the character of God, the God so seen is the one whose heart is moved with pity for the crowd, feeding every last one to overflowing (Matt 15:30f). There are other possible lenses for looking, of course, but I am an Advent person, claimed by this image of the Advent banquet as the promised outcome of all history. In choosing the menu, God specializes in deserts. He sends out engraved invitations, personally delivering them to folks living in poverty trailers and feeding from dumpsters behind the local supermarket. And when these marginal folks arrive, I suspect they will be seated as guests of honor. And those who never doubted being honored at the head table, these will discover that they are assigned to kitchen duty.

Yet again we must ask—what are we to make of those passages about burning and devouring and crushing? Years ago as a student I put this matter straight to my seminary professor: "Do you believe in hell?" "Well," he pondered, "since ours is a God of love, I have a hard time believing in hell. But I do believe in purgatory. Otherwise how can my friend Adolph Hitler come to be reconciled with his brother and sister Jews? For some folks this will likely feel like hell." He had a fine Advent lens.

3. ADVENT WARM-UP

For those of us who like music of all kinds, rock concerts can be exciting happenings. Essential is the warm-up band, contracted to bring anticipation of the main act to a fever pitch. So it is in the Christian year. Advent is a key warm-up event. John the Baptist is the warm-up artist, and his favorite song is "Prepare ye the way of the Lord." His segment of the event permits no passive watching, for his on-stage prophetic gyrations draw us into his water show, only later to recognize that it is only a foreshadowing of a baptism by fire. The scene into which John draws us is radically different from the one being lived outside the arena. Out there in society the beat is aggressive, pitting us against each other in a daily competition to prove ourselves. But here it feels different, luring us to leave such things behind, swaying with upraised hands—just different. Mesmerized, we forget that this isn't the main act—until John crescendos, "Here comes the one whose guitar case I am not even worthy to carry!"

The lights dim, as a solitary spotlight focuses center stage. We wait. We anticipate. But there are no firework bursts, no sequined jumpsuits. Instead, a rather uncomely figure slowly saunters out of the darkness of stage left, with a strange charisma of gentle quietness. Everything is on his terms, and only when he is ready does he sing, and even then, with a whisper. It's a ballad, about treating others as we might like to be treated—with a refrain about being given the courage to walk the walk because we are being called by name, all the while staring at the palm of his hands as if they are written there. Deeply giving all he has to each word, he is drawing us vulnerably out of ourselves, as if into him. The world of buying and selling everything and everybody, the road rage of the Interstate that brought us here, the aggressive parking in the lot outside the arena, all of this begins to feel, well, "quaint." And here inside there is a strange enfolding that invites swaying in the aisles, oblivious to gender or class or ethnicity—together, neighbors as dancing partners. Christmas lights are flashing now, as accompanying guitars swell into an angelic-sounding Gloria—as John the Baptist's former wilderness breaks forth into full bloom. For these sacred moments, thoughts of jealousy and backbiting and anger dissipate into a clapping and singing, cheek turned toward the cheeks of those who once were strangers.

II. LIVING THE SEASONS

All too soon comes the ending. With the feel of an altar call, light and sound diminish as if coalescing into a still point of the turning wheel. Now he is all alone, with just us. He begins a love song, about a community into which we are all invited, where if one cries we all cry, and when if good things happen to one, we all celebrate.

Outside the arena, the night has dampened into a darkly dreary rain. My friend smiles, a bit sadly: "That stuff will never work." "Why not?" "Folks will just take advantage of you." "Maybe." "The world he sings about is pretty, but it isn't the real one—where folks specialize in smacking you on the other cheek." "Probably." "Hey, don't you get sucked into that stuff. You'll end up a loser, just getting hurt!" Still feeling the beat of the music, all I can manage is, "So?" Maybe that's why Christians like to sing. As long as we can hear the beat, we can believe that Advent is the warm-up act for the real thing.

4. WAITING, ALWAYS

One thing I particularly dislike is waiting. It feels like an anxious waste of time—as in standing in the checkout line with nothing to do but stare back at tabloids insisting that Elvis was spotted on Mars. This kind of waiting is the boring kind. But an even worse kind is waiting marinated in fear—like the dentist's waiting room, or at a hospital awaiting the results. Yet there is a third type, one I remember best from childhood—the waiting that is anticipation. It has a delicious agony all its own, as in counting the days and then the hours until Christmas morning.

The four weeks of Advent are all about waiting, involving all three types. Advent can be "boring" in the sense that the church has been waiting for almost 2,000 years for the consummate coming of the one who told us to wait for his return. Scripture ends as a promise: "I am coming soon." Really? And elsewhere: "I go to prepare a place for you." Well how soon is soon! Postponements make waiting dreadfully tiresome.

Advent waiting can also involve "fear" in the sense that Jesus compared his coming to that of a thief in the night, or a master catching with punishment the servant found sleeping. Thus while the good news is that Jesus is coming, the bad news could be that he sounds madder than blazes! But it is the third kind of Advent waiting, as anticipation, that transforms the other two. This kind of waiting is sometimes almost too much—as in a child's Christmas Eve sleeplessness, or the college student's eagerness to return home for a white Christmas.

But it is the aging process in particular that can give such waiting a special sheen. As the years pass, we begin realizing that anticipation is sometimes more preferable than the actualization. The anticipated toy for which we yearned as a child can so quickly be broken, or soon forgotten. A mother's lengthy joy of preparing the Christmas feast surpasses the rapid consumption leading to naps, leftovers, and dirty dishes. The wishing, the hoping, the anticipating—these have a joy all their own. Thus it might be preferable if our adult children not just "drop in," for it deprives us of the joy of anticipation.

Many of us have lost this anticipatory gift that Advent can reignite. Waiting has become relegated to the status of an undesirable protocol for attaining a desirable end. But Advent can invite us into *waiting as a way of life*. Anticipation can give each moment a warm glow, a precious quality for its own its sake. With the first Sunday of Advent, the Christian's "New Year" begins life afresh, rejuvenating our days with the joy of anticipation. While depression is a negative attitude toward nothing in particular and everything in general, so is Advent the contrary. Death-in-life occurs in the person for whom anticipation has been squeezed dry, leaving little more than the remembrance of things past. To regain this Advent attitude, Jesus insists that a child become our model. By becoming childlike, each day can take on the quality of a Christmas Eve, anticipating each fresh morning as being unlike any other that has ever been. Sunset, autumn leaves, frosted trees, the sound of rain. Each time, in every place, with all things, there can be evoked an eagerness of being experienced for the first time, gift wrapped and tagged with one's own name. Picture what it might be like if in this grimly serious society of ours there would be loosen into it Christians restored to Advent playfulness! Heaven is simply a name for imagining when everything might be experienced as *better* than anticipated.

5. ADVENT ANTICIPATION

A friend of mine was a Midwest legend in choral conducting. He introduced his high school students to the whole musical spectrum, from musicals and madrigals to great choral works. He took particular pleasure in discovering students with no claim to obvious talent, and nurturing them to "sing like angels." At the end of each year, he looked forward to a new

II. LIVING THE SEASONS

batch of students, excited over the prospect of performances more perfect than the year before.

Finally he took a late retirement—yet not really. He conducted the "civic singers" and recruited members for an enlarged church choir. But finally his health deteriorated significantly, the doctor's diagnosis being "too many birthdays." Yet when his legs failed, he cherished conducting an annual Christmas program from a chair. And even when moved reluctantly to a care center, he continued to insist on something to which he could look forward. Pushing his walker in front of him, he would beam: "Watch me go all the way to the other side of this room. Tomorrow I'll reach the hall."

But then one night his incontinence brought a defeating humiliation. From that point on, all he could sees was a future of increasing dependence on others, downhill until even his ordinary daily functions would be beyond him to do. "I would rather die," he whispered. And soon he did—going to bed, assuming a fetal position, and refusing either to eat or to speak. The moment when he turned off the life switch of anticipation, he died, even though his body lingered on. There was a large crowd at his funeral, with eulogies praising how well he had lived his life. I kept to myself his final failure—of not having lived well his dying. We buried him during Advent. And after others had left, I stood by his open grave, realizing that he had taught me something important about this season.

Death for him happened when he no longer had anything to which to look forward. So it is with each of us, no matter our circumstances. Freud discovered how deeply within each of us is a "life wish" contending with a "death wish." The death wish prevails when "Good Friday" claims us as the final season. To persevere, the life wish needs Advent. My mother lived her life vicariously through my father. So when he was diagnosed with terminal cancer, she was paralyzed. Her hope was uprooted, for she had no real identity without him. She accomplished her death wish, of dying before he did—hopelessly shriveled to less than seventy pounds.

This makes understandable how Christmases can become lethal for many folks—when the memories of a lost past are permitted to snuff out even the embers of Advent yearning. Sadness comes in remembering childhood Christmases with parents who are now dead. We recall Christmases when we were happily surrounded by our children, children who now have children of their own with whom to spend their Christmases. So why bother to put up even a little tree? With no one to share it, each ball is marinated in sad memories, not worth the risk of being broken. Lost is the

Advent nutrient that feeds the life wish, and in its absence our Christmases are poisoned into a lethal depression.

My friend taught me from the grave that Advent is no incidental season. It is essential to life itself. Advent is the insistence that the heart of Christmas is not about remembering the past, but about celebrating the One who came as a promise of coming again—and again. Advent is for Christmas is for Epiphany is for Lent is for Easter is for Pentecost is for the coming kingdom. And God's promised future is offered with an abundance of gift-wrapped foretastes.

Thus even the tiniest Christmas tree in the smallest of solitary apartments by a terminally ill widow is more than ample witness to an anticipated new heaven and earth. Awakened to see with Advent eyes, she and we can see from the window a cosmos already trimmed, with galaxies as tinsel, planets as balls, and the Milky Way as garland—as she chuckles to herself that with Gabriel on trumpet, the Drummer Boy no longer needs to play solo. Advent is our invitation to peek between the banisters into the living room of God's glory. What we need is not a new landscape but new eyes.

What, then, would I have wanted for my conductor friend? For one thing, I wish that he could have trusted his abundant Advent yearning to the end, realizing that even his best performances were still only hints of a promised "more." I would like to believe that he knows that now. If so, then God has likely assigned him to discern in each new class of recruits those who are without claim to obvious talent—happily nurturing them to sing like angels.

6. ADVENT ARROW

I spend one week each month at the Trappist monastery, and one of those times I was given a heavy responsibility. You need to understand that baking 28,000 fruitcakes is what pays our bills. My assignment centered on the UPS man who comes every weekday of the year to see if we have any fruitcakes to send out to customers. The procedure has been for the driver to stop his truck, enter the bakery, look for someone to tell him if there are any cakes to send, and, if so, where they are. Being the kindly folk we try to be, my assignment was to create a sign that simplifies directions for the poor man. You need to realize how complex this task could be! Not only does the sign need to indicate if there are cakes to be sent, but he needs to know whether he should come in the side door for the few or to the back dock for the many. One could tremble at such a demanding assignment. Our whole bakery industry might depend on my prowess—and maybe even the stability of the UPS franchise!

So what was I to do? If I cut out wooden letters sufficient to spell out all the options, the sign might cover the whole outside wall of our bakery. By morning I was inspired. On one side of a foot square piece of wood I cut and glued these simple letters: "UPS—NO." On the other side: "UPS—YES." Ingenious, but I was only half done. I cut out a red arrow. On the "yes" side, if the arrow is hung pointing down, the driver would know to come to the side door where the sign is hung, maybe with a cup of coffee; and if pointed horizontally to the right, he was to come to the back dock—with or without coffee.

Perfect, but as I was savoring my masterpiece, the abbot startled me. "Something has come up; we need you to be priest tomorrow morning for the second Sunday of Advent." It was late afternoon. With speckles of red paint still on my fingers, and a bit frantic, I skimmed the lectionary Scriptures. Eureka. My sign-making may have actually been a sermon preparation. I resisted making UPS stand for "U Persist in Sin," although that could have functioned as John the Baptist's Advent sign calling for repentance. Instead, I began my Advent homily by suggesting that even if the signs around us seem to indicate God's face turned to "no," faith means persisting in the hope that in returning tomorrow the "yes" side may be face up.

During our youth, I observed, we most often experience the arrow as pointing us further on, toward the future, toward the cornucopia of possibility of a Christmas dock. In middle age, the arrow tends to point down, calling us to taste what we already have. The midlife crisis comes in believing that the arrow points backwards, into the empty sadness of what we shouldn't have done, and what we might have been—with a whiff of unredeemable failure. Depression and despair are the result of obsessive thoughts of having to return empty-handed by the same route we came.

The day's readings were all by Advent folk, using their arrows in full awareness of our dual needs—for side door foretastes that the Lord is good, and the horizontal promise of what awaits around the corner, for "without vision the people perish." Their Advent arrows were likewise painted blood red, as if hyphenating Advent with Lent—much as packing slips relate to invoices. Above all their Advent focus was in disclosing God as a poet who specializes in igniting imaginations. Psalm 72 overflowed with the Advent promise of a peace that shall "abound until the moon shall be no more."

Isaiah's arrow also pointed toward the back dock, where "they shall not hurt or destroy any more." Yet he cheated with two arrows, the other pointing down in prefiguring the vision at the side door where the poor, needy, and meek can receive now (Isa 11:1ff). The New Testament readings reinforce our need for two arrows. The first points to our side door preparation in baptism (Matt 3:1f) in which Christ's Spirit draws each "I" into a "we." Unless this happens so that our craving to "get" is healed into a desire to "share," we will not deal well when directed to the dock (Rom 15:4f).

Advent is prescient of when the "yes" sign will be nailed permanently into place, and there will no longer be need of any arrow. And on the dock the gift-wrapped packages will have name tags for the leopard and the kid, the calf and the lion, the cow and the bear, the lion and the ox, and the little child will show how to open them. By then we shall all have acquired a taste for fruitcakes.

I will not likely be assigned to such a monumental project ever again. But it is enough just to be chosen to hang out the Advent sign for the morning driver.

7. CHRISTMAS SHOPPING—YUCK

Let me be up front about it. For many years in my life I had a downright aversion to Christmas shopping. Since many folks apparently enjoy it, one Advent I asked myself point blank what was the matter with me. Was I afraid of being rejected for getting the wrong present for the right person, or was it the reverse? I just didn't know, so I decided it was time to take a calculated field trip to improve my Advent attitude. To dodge the weekend crowd, I try the mall on a Monday. It doesn't work. Even in the parking lot I hear "Rudolph" and "Silent Night" merging to a rock beat, and the first thing I see on entering is one of Santa's reindeer glistening like Israel's golden calf. I hold out hope that at least a Salvation Army brass quartet might be playing carols. But, alas, they too have disappeared, leaving a solitary volunteer bell ringer and a ghetto blaster with a canned imitation. The words "Merry Christmas" too are gone, replaced by an innocuous "Season's Greetings." And as a final indignity, it turns out that even Santa Claus has been exiled. "Good grief," I mutter with Charlie Brown, what is Christmas without at least a few "Ho, ho, hoes"!

Somewhere between men's underwear and the power drills, I get to thinking about that jolly old fellow. Actually he hasn't been exiled at all, or

II. LIVING THE SEASONS

even demoted to assistant stock boy in the warehouse. Anonymously he has taken over the whole show. When I was a child, St. Nick had his very own domain called "Toyland." Every department store had one, and there he was, smack-dab in the center, on a throne no less. And parents forced each of us children into a frightening yearly liturgy. Eliciting terror akin to a dentist's chair, Santa motioned that I was next for climbing up onto his fat lap. I knew his horrific question by heart: "Have you been good this year?" Early on some kids at school taught me the fine art of lying in such an ambush—white ones. But deceit, even when practiced, is scary business.

One particular year this primal dread returned with a vengeance. This had not been one of my better years. Unquestionably I was in first place on Santa's "naughty list." The jig was up. I knew that he knew—the whole bit, from painting the cat's tail to tormenting the little girl next door at every opportunity. I dodged his eye, but I knew that he was looking straight through me. My tears were a silent "no" even before the question that he didn't ask. He didn't have to. This would surely be a piece-of-coal Christmas, as we were traditionally threatened in Appalachia.

Ominous were the Advent days from that day of reckoning on. For the first time in my life, I stayed in bed on Christmas morning. My parents came to see if I was sick. I might have been. Glumly I descended the stairs, one reluctant step at a time. I don't actually remember what was under the tree. That didn't matter. What mattered was my astonishment that there was anything there for me at all! That was the Christmas I learned that this Santa stuff had it all backwards. Christmas has nothing to do with being rewarded for being good. At its heart it is about a Jesus who comes as a total surprise, because in fact none of us have been very good!

Years later, here I am, being jostled by the frenzied ritual of buying and selling—and suddenly I am gifted in recalling that special morning from my youth. That *is* what Christmas is to be all about: being gifted in spite of our unworthiness. Christmas is like the Eucharist—cupping one's hands like a manger and humbly holding them out to receive the Christ child about which we have just confessed, "Lord, I am not worthy to receive you . . . ." That is why Christmas shopping is such a drag for me. With folks assuming that they deserve to receive presents, they place me under obligation to meet their expectations. It feels like a wedding invitation that "suggests" a website on which to find "appropriate gifts" with price ranges. How can expectations be *gifts*? That's the yuckiness—of living in a world of expectations and obligations rather than one of gracious hospitality. At one of the counters is an advertisement that perhaps hints of an alternative, portraying a husband actually surprising his wife on Christmas. But on reading the finer print, I discovered otherwise. Surely her emotion was one of shock, for the price of the diamond was more than their budget could possibly afford.

So as I sit here in the mall beside the artificial petunias, I compose a new script if ever they reinstate Santa. "Have you been good?" "Yes." "Come on, kid, who are you trying to fool?!" Then, in the midst of the tears comes a hug of surprise, with a whisper: "I haven't either, but let's be sorry together. I love you. It's okay, really!"

That was the Advent Monday I began enjoying Christmas shopping. I tore up my list of things that family and friends had hinted they wanted. Instead I went looking for the toy department.

8. HALF EMPTY, HALF FULL, AND SO WHAT?

Yesterday during my regular venture into the city on errands, I was taken by the interesting sampling of humankind I encountered. At the garage where I got an oil change as Christmas gift for my car, the lady at the desk was downright crotchety. In contrast, the lady waiting for her car was delightful. She was on a cell phone interviewing someone in California so as to be able to sell her one of her homemade dolls. As it turned out, she tries to create a doll face to match the personality of the person ordering the doll. The lady at the desk would not have liked the result.

Moving down the street, the cell phone office seemed hopeless, perhaps because most of the clerks had red noses and sniffled. In contrast, the man in the farm supply store happily shared his wisdom about rubber versus plastic hoses, encouraged by my comment that being a hose expert must be an interesting life's vocation. I declined his offer of an elementary course in nozzles, but somewhere between the bagged salt and the chicken feeders, a theory asserted itself. Folks seem to come in two basic brands, distinguishable as to whether they see life's glass half empty or half full.

I set out to test my thesis at Walmart. But watching from a bench as people came and went proved inconclusive. So during a break in customers, I asked the nearby checkout clerk if she was annoyed at hearing the dinger sound all day long. "Not really; it sounds Christmassy—you know, like jingle bells." This led to a short dialogue when I asked why her dinger was in the D Major range while the one at the grocery outlet seemed closer

II. LIVING THE SEASONS

to an F sharp. Content that her glass was at least half full, I wandered toward the optometrist alcove. Since he had no customers, we chatted about the fine art of finding the right glasses for different shaped noses. When his sense of humor qualified him as a "half-fuller" too, I began to question my thesis. To settle the matter, I moved into the middle of the gift-buying frenzy.

Within half an hour, I had collected considerable data. The half-full folks seem drawn toward interesting things that most others folks seemed to have no interest in buying. The half-empty ones seemed to congregate with sharpened elbows around the things that professed to be on sale. Yet I suspended my final conclusions until encountering the checkout line. My hospitable smile cast toward the man in front of me earned a sobering scowl, as if intent on shriveling anyone within visual range. On the other hand, the lady behind me who was purchasing a tube house for a cat apparently found helpful my information that she would have to supply her own animal. She nicely promised to do so, asking what color I might suggest. On the way home I sophisticated my division of humankind: there are those who "find joy in whatever" and those "suspicious no matter what."

That same evening my thesis found solid confirmation in the day's lectionary Scriptures. The one from the Song of Songs was clearly half full: "Arise my beloved, the winter is past, the rains are over, and the flower appears." To accommodate the half-empty folk, it might read: "Spring will never come; the path is all muddy; but it doesn't matter because flowers just turn brown." But the psalmist persisted, exuding: "Shout for joy . . . be renewed in love . . . sing a new song." Not to neglect the rest of the world's population, I produced a rendition for them: "No thanks; been there, done that; you hear one song, you've heard them all." The Gospel account rendered Zachariah as a head-on half-empty icon. Although God offers him a promise too good to refuse, he is suspicious even of an angel. As a result, he becomes mute, the way such persons tend to be when they are not complaining. Then came the episode with Mary, a full-blown half-fuller all the way: "Let it be done to me!" And off she trots, into the hill country all by herself, totally trusting. Not once does she worry that Elizabeth might be a half-empty type, greeting her with a "You're going to stay with me how many months???" No wonder the two infants in their respective half-full wombs leapt for joy.

Just before I dropped off to sleep, I surmised that these contrasting attitudes have something to do with whether one can trust promises—and thus the future. We are dealing here with a state of mind and not a condition of the world; an orientation of soul rather than a conclusion of mind. It has something to do with believing that if one shows up and does one's best with a smile, the Christmas dawn will somehow happen. And even if it doesn't, one grin beats four grimaces in any hand.

By morning I found my thesis being illustrated everywhere I looked. In a magazine I picked up to read during breakfast, there was a glaringly half-empty editorial. "We must be willing," it insisted, "to sacrifice whatever of our human rights it takes in order to be certain that our stores and streets are free of terrorists." With the morning mail a half-full letter provided my needed balance. It was from my aunt, describing my tiny niece's pre-Christmas (Advent) gift of visiting Disneyland. As they rounded a corner, there he was! She ran and threw herself into his arms, exclaiming, "Mr. Mouse, I've been wanting to meet you all my life. I knew that some day you would come."

I was ready for Christmas. From the mouth of a child had come the yearly call to us half-empty folk to blow on the coals of our Advent yearnings. I was ready to put up my crèche, having heard the script by which a childlike heart can address the manger on Christmas morning. Actually, whether half empty or half full, Christmas is about thankfulness for having a cup. "God, I've been wanting to meet you all my life. I knew that some day you would come."

9. ADVENT CONDUCTING

I still remember my disappointment when some years ago I was invited to the home of an accomplished symphony conductor. Anticipating that together we would listen to some of his favorite music, I even guessed which he might choose. As it turned out, his love was not really of music—but for the accolades awarded him as a conductor. His cherished recordings were restricted to his own performances.

Obsession with the need for recognition can undermine our doings—pollution by the "I." This is why I am uneasy about Scripture passages that attempt to motivate us by promising that "great will be your reward in heaven." Pianists intent on attaining acclaim for technique rather than losing themselves in a Beethoven sonata—these are performers and not musicians, lovers of self more than of music. Analogously, Christians whose motivation for "loving" is in order to bankroll their own heavenly accounts

II. LIVING THE SEASONS

are not Christians as much as contestants, not lovers but users—focused on self rather than God. Keen is the proposal by the eighth-century poet Rabi'a that we "put out the fires of Hell, and burn down the rewards of Paradise. They block the way to God. I do not want to worship from fear of punishment or for the promise of reward, but simply for the love of loving God." The purpose of music is Music, the goal of love is Love, and the "remuneration" for being faithful is God. "Reward" is in the doing, and the gift is in the wanting. Nothing more, nothing less. The love of God is for the sake of loving God.

I confess that my first hint of this way of living emerged from my boyhood love of the Pittsburgh Pirates. Within one month into each season, the only question remaining was by how many games would my beloved "Bucs" end up in last place. Mets fans of old, and certainly the diehards in the center field bleachers at Wrigley Field, they understand. All that really matters is loving the game for its own sake. We real fans are not drawn to the prima donnas who play for the money and the show. It's the utility infielders who play simply because they love the feel of throwing a ball, running the bases, gripping a bat. The position doesn't matter, just so they can play. The sound of a ball well stroked, a double play executed to perfection—these cannot be described, just savored. You either feel it or, well, they shouldn't even let you buy a hotdog.

Such are the analogies that point toward Advent living. My spiritual director described the difference between him and me this way. "I'm eager to reach heaven, while you delight in sampling every wild strawberry along the path." Yes! When his brother died, he confessed envy that he was not the one "called home" for his "eternal reward." Not me. I hope my invitation gets lost in the mail, or at least that I can find a detour. While he can't wait for the "real thing," I have more Advent foretastings to practice. The best Advent banner may be the one raised mid-season by the perennially hopeful Cubby loyalists: "Wait Till Next Year!"

There is nothing quite like Advent hope—having about it the infield greenness of earth's rebirth just about the time spring training begins; and the smell of burning autumn leaves around the time the "boys in October" do their thing—hopefully without the Yankees. Being teased into foretaste by Advent hope—that's what it's about, so much so that I might be tempted to return the rain check if there are no Advents in heaven.

When my conductor friend died, he still hadn't "gotten it." Yet I am hopeful that God has an orchestra waiting for him, with one crucial directive: that he prepare for a "concert" in which there will be no audience, and there will be no recording. This may take numerous rehearsals before he "gets it." But when he does, they will play together forever, "rehearsing" for no other reason than as an excuse to make music for the sheer joy of it. I recently experienced a church in which various members take turns playing music, all day and all night, without an audience, for God. What an Advent anticipation of when there will be "myriads of myriads and thousands of thousands, singing with full voice, 'Worthy is the Lamb . . .'" (Rev 5:12–13 RSV).

10. ADVENT FORGIVENESS

Particularly interesting is the third Sunday of Advent called "Gaudete Sunday." It is the parallel of "Laetare Sunday" that falls on the fourth Sunday of Lent. Both are Latin names meaning "rejoice." While the liturgical color for both of these two seasons is a pensive purple, these two special days within the seasons are adorned a childlike flavor of pink. Waiting for both Christmas and Easter seemed unbearable at times for me as a child. So my parents acquiesced to my eagerness and gave me one Christmas gift to open in advance, and one bag of Easter jellybeans to devour in preview. Something of this idea is behind these two special Sundays, lightening the mauve atmosphere with an anticipatory sampling.

They are days tailored for pondering about what in one's life might be the deepest reason for "rejoicing." Since earliest times, the church has encouraged repentance issuing in confession as the appropriate preparation for the rejoicing—much as a shower before dressing for a special occasion. Purple symbolizes this preparation through repentance, and its intersection with pink anticipates the forgiveness. While many denominations and scores of Christians now neglect this essential process, the ubiquitousness of Alcoholics Anonymous's twelve-step program is proving how essential this practice is. Drugs, obesity, pornography, on and on—this widespread expansion of foci is witnessing to the need that each of us has to acknowledge something for which "we can't but God can." This first step then deepens into a "searching and fearless inventory" concerning how each of us with our particular Achilles heel has hurt other persons (Step 4). What follows is a confessing "to God, to ourselves, and to another human being the exact nature of our wrongs" (Step 5). Then, in receiving forgiveness as the primal gift that is Christmas and Easter, we are enabled to make "direct

II. LIVING THE SEASONS

amends" in healing the hurts that we have caused—as symbolized in the celebrations of Epiphany and Pentecost. Step 10 is the ongoing promise to continue this "personal inventory" and reconciliation for the rest of one's life. In other words, Advent is a lifetime venture.

Some years ago I conducted a workshop for thirty ministers in which I tested this understanding. I asked each person to write on an unsigned piece of paper either the word "yes" or "no" as answer to this question: "Is there anything in your past that if known would likely discredit your ministry?" The anonymous tabulation? Thirty "yeses." Subsequent workshops have confirmed this statistic. The Christian dynamic of confession, forgiveness, and restitution, far from being a life practice reserved for "addicts," is a dynamic essential in becoming fully human. "Originating sin" characterizes us all. Above all, then, what should distinguish the church from society is not the absence of sin but the acknowledgement of our condition, refusing to pretend it away as "mistakes" or "indiscretions." Advent is about the healing of sin, ongoingly.

Recently the Sisters of Loretto erected a monument at their Mother House in Kentucky honoring the slaves whom over a century ago they had owned and buried anonymously in the far end of their cemetery. At the dedication, the prioress pleaded guilt. "We cannot undo the sins of the past, but we can confess them, and request forgiveness—even though asking is one of the most difficult things we have to do." In truth she was speaking for each Christian and for every church—for no other religion has claimed such lofty principles, and none other has failed so badly in living up to them.

This is why a worship service without confession and forgiveness can hardly claim to be Christian. Without serious Advent preparation, "rejoicing" can be little more than a trifling happy time—for we are blind to the profound need to be gifted. I was quite young when I heard a poem at Vacation Bible School that I knew even then that I needed to memorize. It had to do with a child coming sorrowfully to the teacher's desk at lesson's end, asking for a new page, "for I have spoiled this one." The teacher, in turn, approaches God's throne, asking for a new life, "for I have spoiled this one." In both cases, the gift is granted, with the same response: "Do better now my child." Christmas is not just for children, but for all of us who are becoming childlike through Advent humbling.

REASONS FOR THE SEASONS

11. ADVENT AS GRACIOUS STERILITY

During these final days of Advent an interesting sub-theme emerges from the lectionary readings. From the Old Testament we encounter a couple who, although barren, gives birth to the strong man Samson. The New Testament reading presents us with a sterile couple who, nonetheless, gives birth to the strong precursor, John the Baptist. On a subsequent day, we read of Hannah who, though sterile, gives birth to the strong prophet Samuel. The accompanying Psalm promises that a barren wife will bear seven sons. These instances are only a few of the many stories appearing throughout Scripture that reinforce this theme of sterility—Sarah, Rebekah, Rachel, right up to Mary, who as a virgin incapable of bearing a child yet gives birth the strong redeemer of all creation.

With such a number of cases, one might think that God is running a problem pregnancy clinic. And indeed that is the point. "Hail, Mary, full of Grace, the Lord is with you." Grace is the word best characterizing the heart of the good news—that we are gifted in our nothingness by the graciousness of God's immeasurable generosity. Did Samson's parents do anything to deserve being gifted? No, they were ordinary folks. What about the parents of John the Baptist? No, the father was just a regular priest. What of Hannah? No again, just a simple peasant woman. Well, then, surely Mary! No, just a poor unknown teenager of "low estate."

Thus while Advent is a time in which we prepare to *give* gifts to others, it is more deeply the time of the year for learning and relearning how to *receive* gifts. Sterility is the condition of emptiness without which we cannot truly receive. Jesus Christ comes as a Christmas gift, or not at all. Clutching or "deserving" hands cannot receive it. Christianity is about the miracle of the empty hands, with sad eyes closed—and reopened into the wide-eyed wonder of a child.

Christmas makes the syntax of Advent clear. The syntax of Advent living is never a matter of *if* you do, *then* God will—as if we can ever deserve God's love. The syntax of Christmas is *because* God has, *therefore* you can. We are freed from ourselves by being so freely gifted that we become gracious through the receiving. Advent-Christmas-Epiphany are one hyphenated event. The grammar of renewal into fullness is this threefoldness of unfulfilled longing, gracious gift, and liberation to give as we have received. Advent is a time of humble emptying without which one cannot be surprised by grace. After receiving our Christmas gifting, Epiphany ("Manifest") marks our beginning in beholding everything as gift.

II. LIVING THE SEASONS

During Advent, then, scriptural words such as sterility, barrenness, and infertility are helpful in evoking words that particularize the feel of our own condition—restless, fruitless, unfulfilled, yearning, unproductive, powerless, longing, despondent, inept, insufficient, discounted, unwanted, drained, and threatened. Advent brings clarity that all of us, in some way or another, are living somewhere between "things are all wrong" and "things don't seem quite right." Mary understood this—that the gift-bearing God can only feed "the hungry with good things," and thus as a loving God has "sent the rich away empty," if ever they are to be filled. The Christian God lovingly "lifted up the lonely" and lovingly "brought down the powerful from their thrones" (Luke 1:51–53 NRSV).

This Advent-Christmas dynamic makes explicit what is involved in "falling in love." It is inconceivable for the loved one to mutter, "What took her so long to realize how lovable I am?" No, falling in love is such a gift that one spontaneously marvels, "What on earth does she see in me?" So it is with God. Although we are rarely very lovable, the impossible possibility has happened. God has fallen in love with us. Amazing grace, simply amazing.

12. KEYS AND THE MASKED MAN

As a boy, my favorite radio show happened every Friday at 6:00 o'clock. There was this cowboy who rode into a different town each week, solved the most unjust of dilemmas, and rode away into the sunset shouting, "Hi ho Silver, away!" Always someone would ask, "Who is that masked man?" And always someone in the admiring crowd would acclaim, "Why that's the Lone Ranger!" I would feel a spine tingle, hoping that some Friday we would find out who he really was. Maybe in some future episode a persuasive mayor would present him with a key to the town, and then the local newspaper editor could interview him.

So it was with Jesus. He would enter a town (once with a brown donkey, but never on a white horse), solve their problems, but then move on—leaving the multitudes to ask, in effect, "Who is that masked man?" Not surprisingly, then, even after Jesus disappeared for good, people have continued to ask that same question. "Who is he—really?" Almost immediately, his admirers searched the Old Testament for hints and promises that might expand his identity. Soon the early church collected these treasured guesses, and, as we shall see, were intent on singing them during the final week of Advent—"Emmanuel," "Wisdom," "Lord," "Root," "Dawn," "King," and "Key." This latter one I find particularly intriguing—Jesus as the "Key of David." Isaiah first provided that metaphor: "I will place on his shoulder the key of the house of David; he shall open, and no one shall shut; he shall shut and none shall open" (Isa 22:22 RSV). The book of Revelation absorbed this image and insisted that Christ, in possessing the key of David, sets before us "an open door, which no one is able to shut" (Rev 3:8 RSV).

What is this crucial door? It is the door of doors—the one between us and God, between time and eternity, between earth and heaven, between death and life. Once we recognize this, we are offered a wonderfully gentle invitation. "Behold I stand at the door and knock; if anyone hears my voice and opens the door, I will come in to him and eat with him, and he with me" (Rev 3:20 RSV). To shift the analogy a bit, this knock discloses our human dilemma—the door would seem to be locked and we are keyless. To be finite is to feel locked in. And while Christ has the key, it works only from the outside. Yet his is a "skeleton key," able is open any lock, but it is in the shape of a cross.

I belonged to an inner city Christian commune in the 1960s that was keen on poverty and recycling. We found an old door in a dumpster, put legs on it, and there it was—our dining room table. Someone suggested that Christ had not only unlocked our door, but had taken off its hinges—making it the very table where he promised to eat with us and we with him. Thus each meal was to be a mini-holy communion. And as the neighborhood poor began to accept our invitation, our table kept expanding. It felt like an insignificant thing to do. And yet "when was it that we saw you hungry and gave you food, or thirsty and gave you something to drink?" (Matt 25:37 NRSV). What we slowly began to experience was that it was the poor who were the knocking of Christ, and the open door was into an extended family. "Just as you did it to one of the least of these who are members of my family, you did it to me" (v. 40).

I often wondered what motivated the Long Ranger to go around doing good. I never knew. But I have learned the "why" of God's "Masked Man"— a "why" so powerful that his knocking persists in the face of unanswered doors, insistent even at doors slammed in his face. The Advent annunciation gives us an amazingly sensuous clue. Dare we call it religious pornography? A bewildered Mary quizzes the angel about her promised pregnancy. "How can this be" since I have never had intercourse? But you will, responds Gabriel—with God! The language used is quite suggestive. God the Holy Spirit

II. LIVING THE SEASONS

"will come upon you," upon her, over her, in her—by which "the power of the Most High will overshadow you" (Luke 1:35 NRSV). To these discreetly chosen words, Mary succumbs: "Here am I . . . let it be . . ." (v. 38). The Key of David unlocked the womb of Mary and disclosed God's love affair with humanity. God has fallen in love with us!

Some friends bought land with an abandoned barn to begin a Christian commune. In it they found an old sheep manger, and made it their altar. What symbolism—gathering around a manger of Christ's birth to be fed as children born of his divine-human love affair. On the open stable door for his expanding family, Christ has written these blood-red Advent words: "Please Keep Open."

13. WEARY AND WEARIED

When the Lectionary Scriptures for Advent begin repeating themselves, it's time for us to take notice. Five times in one week we hear these words by Isaiah: "Is it too little for you to weary mortals, that you weary my God also?" (Isa 7:13 NRSV). Significantly, Advent climaxes around the time of the Winter solstice—the shortest day and the longest night. Abbreviated days often bring weariness as we try to squeeze in all that needs doing before dark. Even more, the length of the nights can bring weariness about life itself. Darkness often feeds the loneliness with life-draining memories. Haunted by a past that is departed but haunts, apprehensive of a future that is unlikely, the present can become scarred with anxiety. Some churches are beginning to recognize this irony—that Advent, intended to bring anticipatory joy, is in fact the season of most suicides. These congregations offer a "Service of Shared Sadness" where persons huddle together in the weary Advent darkness, finding solace through the companionship of common grieving.

Recently I shared with a fellow monk how much we can learn about each other by noting the recurring theme of our prayers during Mass. "Do you know," he asked, "the petition you pray most often?" I confessed ignorance. "For the lonely." He knows me. As an extrovert only child raised by introvert parents, this concern has deep autobiographical roots. I had an invisible friend, and one dog. The one grew tired of me, the other died. And so began my long spiritual pilgrimage toward belonging.

Last Christmas I was gifted with an amazing book of photographs taken from by the Hubble telescope. I became delightfully lost in the dancing beauty of whirling galaxies within galaxies. Yet when I shared it with a friend, he shuttered, forcefully closing the book. "What I feel in those pictures," he whispered, "is the loneliness of being a forgotten speck, abandoned among endless light years of cold emptiness." That night as I walked in the joy of Advent silence beneath a full moon upon dazzling fresh snow, I ached remembering my childhood, and my friend. And for all who at that very moment were experiencing this same moon but for whom it was a harbinger of that loneliness when coyotes wail and the insane scream. Through my pilgrimage I have been drawn upwardly into praise of a God whose wholesale business is the creating of our awesome cosmos. Yet these cold Advent nights can make one less certain about God's retail trade—the part about so knowing each fallen sparrow by name and counting the hairs of our heads that he is in the engraving business, carving our names into the palms of his hands.

An important night in my Advent pilgrimage happened when my hermitage was swept by an intense hail storm, plunging everything into total darkness. In an instant I was stripped of lights, heat, water pump, refrigerator, stove—and shortly thereafter the telephone went dead. Seconds of waiting passed into minutes, minutes into an hour, and an hour opened out into a totally uncertain future. There was little left to do but stumble up the dark stairs to bed. Wrapped in extra blankets, I waited, shivered, and just waited. The dead clock rendered time timeless, and I sleepless. That was the night for sensing how deeply this eerie physical uncertainty resembles the darkness that thousands upon thousands of persons were experiencing psycho-spiritually at that same moment. Helpless, wrapped in darkness, with only the vagueness of weary waiting for nothing. "My only companion," cried out the Psalmist, "is darkness" (Ps 88:18 Grail).

I was left in that immobile state for three days. When electricity was finally restored, my hunger was to grasp outside of myself. Quickly scrolling the accumulated email, I was surprised by the name of an acquaintance from long ago. Curious, I opened it. And within a few words, she plunged me into her weary darkness of narrowing options—early abuse by her father, a messy divorce, abandonment by a lover, impairment by a stroke, lost job, and now a final alienation from her daughter. "There's nothing left, and I am so weary that I am not even sure that I have the strength for suicide." There was no phone number. What can one possibly say in an email sufficient to bequeath Advent hope for a life drained to the dregs?

II. LIVING THE SEASONS

I recalled that Advent passage from Isaiah: "Is it too little for you to weary others, that you weary my God also?" Her version had a further twist. "Is it too little for you, God, in wearying others to weary me beyond endurance unto death?" I recalled the Lectionary psalm that accompanied the Isaiah passage. It inquired as to who could leave this valley of the shadow of death to "ascend the hill of the Lord?" The answer? "Those who have clean hands, and pure hearts, who do not lift up their souls to what is false" (Ps 24:4 NRSV). With requirements such as these, the path must be covered with weeds.

I reread the Isaiah passage. The context was a king who when confronted by a threatening enemy felt so hopeless that "his heart and the heart of his people shook as the trees of the forest shake before the wind" (Isa 7:2 RSV). Thus when Isaiah asked him what sign of hope he would need in order to quench his despair, like most of us, he hadn't a clue. Surely this is what Joseph felt in the accompanying Gospel reading when he learned that his beloved Mary was pregnant, and he was not the father. Only God knows what sign each of us needs in order to hope again. Yet the one he gave Joseph touches the deepest craving of the human soul—the assurance that God's very identity is Emmanuel, "God *with* us." Always.

I realized then that this was precisely what my suicidal friend was inwardly screaming to hear. The reason she had written me was the hope against hope that she was not alone—that someone somewhere sometime cared whether she was alive and not dead. I cared, and would say so. But surely this would have little staying power unless through my words she could hear God's Advent retail promise, that "I will never forsake you. See, upon the palms of my hands I have written your name" (Isa 49:16 NAB). Even more, through Christ comes the realization that our names have been written there with nails, using blood as ink. Jesus's final words say it all: "I am with you always . . ." (Matt 28:20 RSV). I knew then how to begin my Advent email to her: "My Dear friend, you are not alone . . . ."

14. O COME, O COME—ANYHOW, ANYWAY!

There is a beautiful tradition used for centuries by many churches and monastic orders for structuring the final week of Advent. As we mentioned, it draws names from various scriptural prophecies identifying the One who is to come. Each title is given an Advent feel with the prefix "O" as the soft sound of yearning. Appropriately they are called the "O antiphons," singing one each evening at Vespers as a way of fashioning a particular tone of anticipation for the following day. Many of us know these antiphons, probably unknowingly, because they provide the choruses for the well-known Advent hymn, "O Come, O Come Emmanuel." By singing one stanza each day of this final week, we are joined in the great chorus of Advent worshippers down through the ages.

December 16. "O Come Emmanuel" is the first verse, celebrating God's promise through Isaiah that a child shall be born for us whose name is Emmanuel, "God with us."

December 17. "O Wisdom" declares that the child who is to be born in a mangered disguise will be none other than God's companion through whom the very heavens and earth are being spoken into being.

December 18. "O Sacred Lord" uses Israel's favorite word for referring to God, thereby insisting that the coming Savior is the face of very God of very God.

December 19. "O Root of Jesse" acknowledges the royal humanity of this coming Messiah, born in the lineage of Jesse, the father of King David.

December 20. "O Key of David" declares that just as King David held the keys to Israel's kingdom, so Jesus will bring the keys to unlock the mystery of the cosmos as entry into the promised kingdom of God.

December 21. "O Radiant Dawn" identifies Jesus as the one who will bring the new beginning that Zechariah prophesized, for he is the One who in the "gentle compassion of our God" shall "break upon us" with "the dawn from on high."

December 22. "O King of all the Nations" promises that with Christ will begin the peaceable kingdom—that "new heaven and new earth" when the wolf and lamb shall feed together and war shall be no more.

December 23. "O Come Emmanuel" repeats the first O antiphon so as to connect promise with fulfillment, the first with the last—for the God who in the beginning created all things is the same God who will bring them to completion in becoming "All in all."

December 24. Augustine is so right, that by singing the Scriptures we pray them twice. Thus prepared, Advent's eager awaiting moves toward its crescendo in the most precious of all eves.

II. LIVING THE SEASONS

15. CHRISTMAS EVE TRUST

The very name "Christmas Eve" has a magic all its own. Perhaps this is because so many of the days of our living seem wrapped in a somber Advent mood rather than emitting a Christmas flavor. In the same way, many of us are not Easter folks very often, spending most of our time in the Holy Saturday range. Expressed another way, we are usually "in-between persons," suspended somewhere between Advent and Christmas, between Good Friday and the resurrection. While this could warrant God's judgment of us that we are neither cold nor hot but lukewarm (Rev 3:15–16 RSV), there is a way in which this "in-betweenness" expresses Christian living at its best.

One Christmas as a youth I went all the way and risked asking Santa for a bicycle. The frequencies of my parental reminders were simply compensatory covers for my doubt about ever getting one. What I remember most about all this was not the skinned knees on Christmas Day when I tried to tame the thing. What I remember most is what I felt on that extended Christmas Eve when at dawn I stood motionless on the staircase landing. I braced myself for the final step into knowing, when I could peep through the banisters into the living room, and know, one way or the other. My tender years trembled with an eagerness wrapped in doubt, a hope teased by uncertainty. The frightening eagerness of one more step—when doubt would evaporate, yet hope might be dashed.

Looking back now, I realize that such moments are portents of life experienced at its deepest level. The heart of Christian living entails the delicious anxiety of being poised on the edge—unable to wait yet apprehensive about acting. What happened after that moment? I looked, I embraced, I rode, I fell—and it became my companion. But it is that "magical edge" between Christmas Eve and Christmas Day that remains singular. As my suspicions about Santa Claus grew into confirmation, my trust in my parents became wounded, for they had lied to me about Christmas. In a way, it marked my entrance into lost innocence—into an evolving enmeshment in doubts, as time threatened to demythologize my hopes and dreams into blandness.

Yet, ironically, in becoming a serious Christian, I was gifted with an alternative version of Christmas meaning. Near the end of his life, a famed philosopher, who had struggled much of his life in the search for answers to life's deepest questions, was asked, "If you could begin living your life over again, which option would you choose: to know the answers, or to spend your life struggling with the questions. He quickly chose the latter—and as a Christian, so do I.

I realize that there are Christians who live as if beliefs can wrap them in protective certainty. Yet, in doing so, they forfeit faith—for in denying the struggle with questions and doubts, they become anemic of hope. Faith is never certainty but always wagering, a gambling marinated in the excitement of anticipation. Hope is never surety but is anchored in trusting a promise without proof. It involves desiring what is not logical, believing what might be unlikely, tantalized by what may be too good to be true—choosing the risk of disappointment over placation with little more than the same. Childlikeness is what Jesus called it, flavoring our days with the color of Christmas Eves. As a child, joy needs only a mud puddle or a cardboard box—for every "whatever" is gift-wrapped in possibility. The mangered child is down payment on God's promise to "return"—as those precious Christmas Eve moments on life's landings, on the edge of hoping against hope. These are what tease the hidden child in each of us to live in anticipation, peeking daily through the banisters into God's cosmic living room. More of the same hardly involves risk, but wagering on the vision of Christmas risks hope. In a society lost in tastelessness, we need our Christmas Eves to reignite the liveliness of Christian faith. It means living the tension of "now" but "not yet." Apprehensively eager, hopefully uncertain, the Christian lives poised deliciously on every edge.

16. NOT CHRISTMAS DAY AT ALL

How quickly Christmas is over. The kids break their new toys, or grow tired of them. Grandma begins the dinner by apologizing yet one more time for the lumpy mashed potatoes. Uncle George dominates conversation in repeating his same jokes. Napping after the feast seems to come sooner each year. Been there, done that, but in slower repeat. The writer of Ecclesiastes apparently has been spying in on our Christmases—that there is "nothing new under the sun." Apropos, my local newspaper last week provided this advice: "If you expect this Christmas to be any different than what it has always been, brace yourself for frustration."

Looking backward from Christmas Day, perhaps the focal point of Christmas may not be Christmas Day after all. Since the stores start Christmas even before Thanksgiving, by Christmas Day folks are numb. The very next day, the stores sell off Christmas at sale prices, and overnight the

II. LIVING THE SEASONS

Valentine's Day displays are in place. Yet Christmas at the monastery is different. Nothing of Christmas really appears until Christmas Eve day. A day or two before, several of us with the eagerness of children romp the snow in search for the perfect tree, as others with whetted imagination initiate the decorating. Hallway aromas evoke guessing as to what might be happening in the kitchen. And for four Advent weeks now, our scriptural worship has been progressively an intensification of promise—yet always against a purple backdrop of realism, teasing our hibernated yearnings.

The first sound of a Christmas carol will not be until Vespers on Christmas Eve. On the way to church a large star glows its promise outside over our cloister, and inside the tree is blessed, permitting its lights to glitter for the first time. The Christ child is placed in the manger, as the sound of chant and the smell of pine commingle with the incense of sticky buns baking for devouring after midnight Mass. All is ready. Christmas Eve, the Eve of eves, when yearning becomes gift-wrapped in mystery.

On this night is there anyone in whom there is not at least an ember of hope that things can be different—somehow, sometime, somewhere? In the face of persistent odds to the contrary, struggling deeply to be born within each of us is the hope that the world's tomorrows will not be stamped with endless sameness. Unlike society around us, at the monastery this dynamic does not move toward a crescendo of Christmas morning presents. There are no "presents," for Christmas Eve as the world's foretaste in promise is itself the gift, to overflowing.

Why, then, do our Christmas Days rarely measure up to our Christmas Eves. I find a possible clue in Kazantzakis's novel *Zorba the Greek*. When Zorba encounters an old man planting olive trees that he will never live long enough to enjoy, he asks him "Why? The response: "I act as if I will live forever." Zorba counters, "I act as if each moment will be my last." Somehow they are both right, and together they touch the mystery of Christmas Eve. In drinking deeply each moment as if the final gift, we can experience it in foretaste as if for the first time of forever.

17. CHRISTMAS AT DAWN

I am convinced that Kenneth Graham's classic children's story *The Wind in the Willows* is really a parable for adult children. The story images the world as a pond in which creatures are learning to live together. The beautiful center chapter is entitled "Piper at the Gates of Dawn." The tiny Otter has become lost in the darkness, and none of the animal friends are able to find him. Not until Pan plays his flute in awakening the dawn's gates, flooding with light the path for the Otter's jubilant homecoming.

What a fine image for understanding Jesus. Much of his life, as perhaps ours, was lived in darkness. He was born at night, lived thirty years in the tiny darkness of obscurity, was betrayed at night, died as darkness descended over the whole land, and "while it was still dark" the women came to the empty tomb (John 20:1 RSV). The plight of the disciples in their storm-tossed boat is our story: "It was now dark, and Jesus had not yet come to them" (John 6:17 RSV).

Christmas is about the one who comes in the darkness—as fulfillment and yet as ongoing promise, as once and for all but as one yet to come. Jesus is the flute player awakening the gates of the world's Christmas re-dawning. His music unlocks each door to the sunrise, its lilt promising an opening of graves to a new day of homecoming. "Awake, O harp and lyre! I will awake the dawn" (Ps 108:2 RSV). We all remember as children tossing and turning all night in eagerness for the hint of Christmas dawn, signaling parental permission to go see. Yet even that moment only insinuates the real procession yet to be, when the child in each of us will arise to follow Jesus the childlike Pied Piper, up and down the vales in search of all the otters who would like to be found—and together entering through the gates of the dawn. In deep matters, the call is for poets, not literalists. Then whatever else such a promised homecoming will be like, surely there will be a Christmas tree—a huge one, right in the center.

18. CHRISTMAS AS DEADLY

Unlike the rest of the world, the church firmly rejects the secular one-day Christmas routine. Christmas is so important that it is to be celebrated for twelve days, from Christmas Day until Epiphany. It is so important, indeed, that the church has found creatively ways to celebrate it even in times and places where observance was forbidden. So it was for three centuries in England (1558–1829) when certain groups of Christians were forbidden to practice their faith openly. So, as the story goes, an anonymous person wrote a Christmas carol as a secret catechism for the youth. On the surface it is a harmless fun song, but underneath is a code serving well even today for remembering the richness of our faith.

II. LIVING THE SEASONS

Many of us know this song by heart as "The Twelve Days of Christmas." The partridge in a pear tree (the cross) stands for Jesus as the center of our lives. The "two turtle doves" represent the Old and New Testaments through which the Holy Spirit discloses the meaning of life. The "three French hens" symbolize the three theological virtues of faith, hope, and love as the basis for Christian living. The "four calling birds" stand for the four Gospels from which the gospel is proclaimed. The "five golden rings" represent the Old Testament Law (the first five books of the Bible) that record God's wedding and honeymoon with his people. The "six geese a-laying" stand for the six days of creation as the theatre for our divine-human drama. The "seven swans a-swimming" are the sevenfold gifts of the Holy Spirit: wisdom, understanding, counsel, fortitude, knowledge, piety, and awe of the Lord. The "ten lords a-leaping" symbolize the Ten Commandments as our code of ethical behavior. The "eleven pipers piping" are the eleven faithful disciples who are to be our models. And the "twelve drummers drumming" remind us of the twelve beliefs summarized in the Apostles' Creed.

This richly coded carol is a powerful witness to the countless Christians through the ages who have risked death in order to preserve what for us lies hidden behind Rudolph and the "ho-ho-hoes."

19. CHRISTMAS PAST

We all remember Scrooge from Charles Dickens's *A Christmas Carol*—that miserly and selfish remains of a shriveled person who once was human. His redemption came through the visitation of three ghosts—Christmas Past, Christmas Present, and Christmas Future. Together they form—for not only Scrooge but for all of us—the sequence by which Christmas can become a spiritual encounter. Quiet, now, for the "Ghost of Christmas Past" is about to make his disquieting entrance.

Several years ago I decided that simplifying my home environment would make a good Advent preparation for Christmas. Dusting and rearranging the furniture was the easy part. Then I reached my study. Dominating the room were six huge file drawers crammed with folders going back to graduate school days and beyond. There they stood, hardly ever opened for almost forty years, defiantly glaring at me. Every day of week one I gathered increased determination to glare right back at them. On the second Monday, guilt tipped the scale. Much against my will, I began the weeding process. There were class notes, texts of lectures given, ideas for books I never wrote. Hardest of all was the evocation of personal memories. Love notes from my daughters, cherished letters from friends, special Christmas cards from folks now dead—sprinkled amidst diplomas and awards. I can feel the edge of tears even now. How can one throw away one's past? I cried. It was painful. Then with clinched eyes, I put it all, all of it, into eight huge trash bags. Within half an hour, the ghost of things past had been relabeled as trash, and my hard-earned memories now have residency in the county landfill.

I have pondered much about that day. To a certain extent it feels like a sad and terrible parable of life itself. As the hymn puts it, time is like "an ever-rolling stream" bearing all away. "They fly forgotten . . . ." Yet had I not taken the courage for this act, in time someone else would just have had to do it—they too with tears but with lesser understanding. Sometimes aging feels like death by attrition. Looking backwards from life's fatal finale, all our once frantic doings have but paper-thin substance, faded dreams, as our own bodies shrivel relentlessly in preparation for permanent residency in the cemetery landfill. Embalming was already occurring. Death is not simply what marks the end, but is a red thread woven into the very fabric of life. Obstinate, persistent, unyielding, inexorable, insistent, unrelenting, uncompromising.

The memories of Christmas Past can make one feel like a yellowing photo album, glued with cherished faces destined at one's death to be rendered forever nameless. It can feel like a baseball pitcher who is doing his best, only to glance over at the bull pen where the coach is warming up his replacement. Each year the Christmas tree gets smaller, until it is eventually a miniature plastic one on an end table, symbol of slow death by fading memory. A letter to the editor this week in the local newspaper was an honest confession: "Christmas is a holiday that persecutes the lonely, the frayed, and the rejected."

Scrooge's frantic question becomes ours. Can the negative haunting by the Ghost of Christmas Past be exorcized? Yes, for such pain can lead us into the heart of God. Prayers in Scripture are of two types. In the first, we entreat God *not* to remember—pleading that he drop our sins into the landfill of his forgetting. "Remember not the follies of our youth," sobs the psalmist—not only our long-term ones, but the soilings of this morning's motivations. Yet the stained impact of these past ghosts can be erased permanently from our present life, if only God is so willing. "I so will it," says

II. LIVING THE SEASONS

Jesus. The real Christmas gift is a divine forgiveness that bequeaths new beginnings. Every saint has a forgiven past, each sinner an invited present.

But there is more. Not only do we pray for what we need God to always *forget*, but the second kind of praying is for that which we need God to always *remember*. "Remember me, O Lord . . ." (Ps 106:4 RSV). And God so wills it. This Christmas gift of remembrance is a promise not only that the divine memory will enfold us personally, but that God sorts through our doings with a sense of humor, resurrecting from our past that which is worth preserving. The meaning thread of history is God's memory, that compassionate and refining surveillance in which he delves through the file drawers and albums of our past, salvaging what is worth preserving in his memory bank as grist for his imagination. In this positive sense, our pasts are being resurrected as an ongoing Christmas present, never lost but divinely refined. That which we most fear to lose is likely what is most cherished by God—the laughter, singing, gifts, feasting, snowy Christmas Eves, the whole bit, at its best.

Marcel Proust was obsessed with this loss of the past, and wrote his six-novel classic, *Remembrance of Things Past*, hoping that by recording minutely the nuances of his memory, he could somehow grant immortality to time. Unknowingly, his futile effort was an imitation of God's enterprise. Christian living is rooted in the trust that in each moment God is doing the Advent work of simplification, discarding our undesirable files into his dumpster, weaving the best of our past into God's own ongoing present, treated as precious ornaments for a Christmas future beyond our imaginings. The Ghost of Christmas Past is exorcized by the Spirit of Christmas called Holy.

20. CHRISTMAS PRESENT

Belief in the Christian God, who redeems our pasts by winnowing them into his own becoming, can help us escape the depressive "Ghost of Christmas Past." In so doing, we are gifted with the courage to encounter the "Ghost of Christmas Present." Strange though it may sound, living fully in the *present* is one of the hardest things to do. That is why the four weeks of Advent is training in doing just that—so dealing with our past that we are opened to a joyously ongoing living of Christmas Present. When I shared with a friend my having abandoned my eight bagfuls of past to the trash, he was incredulous: "How on earth does that really make you feel!" "Free!"

I replied, without hesitation. It was hard to explain the resurrecting of my sad memories into promise, but even harder to describe the experience of having my shameful ones trashed. Forgiveness is God's way of liberating us from our past by settling our accounts payable, opening the possibility of living each "Now" without a bottom line recorded in red ink.

This is powerful stuff, evoking Isaiah's lyric celebration of God: "You have cast all my sins behind your back" (Isa 38:17 NRSV). As our gnawing memories are anesthetized in the intimate darkness of the stable, the mangered child opens his eyes, and ours, into the experience of childlikeness—the capacity to live each now as a Christmas. We become ingenious, insouciant, and alacritous—these are the big words for it. The smaller ones are to become serenely centered, innocently playful, and deeply loving—capable of savoring even the tiniest things of our lives as Christmas presents. In fact, both for the child newly born and the adult twice born, simply to be alive is an awesome gift. How wonderful the possibility of experiencing each night with the lilt of a Christmas Eve, anticipating dawn as adorned with surprises worthy of a Christmas Day. With eyes rebaptized to see, ears cleaned to hear, things take on this flavor of giftness—the fragrance of first coffee, the soundlessness of falling snow, cardinals and blue jays coloring the feeder, the humor of becoming impatient in morning traffic—each moment sprightly gift-wrapped.

For this childlike demeanor that is the mindful expectancy characterizing Christmas Present, liberation of two kinds is needed. Not only must we be freed from being sucked back into the futile reliving of our arduous past, but we must be freed from the future as well. Strong is the temptation to postpone our living until later, squandering the richness of each "now" for the sake of a future "someday." Living is delayed until *after* this or *when* that has happened. Even our days are confined by lists of things needing to be done or acquired *before* we are "free" finally to "live," to "be," to "do our thing." Jesus takes exception to this obsession. "Take no thought of the morrow" is Jesus' redemptive alternative, for the future can be both distraction and diversion from the quality of life offered as a mindful present.

After writing this last sentence, I took a break. I walked to the window, and there it was, dawn's "now" gift. Snow had been falling through the night, with no apparent intent of stopping. I was being tested about what I had just written. As I looked out upon the floating beauty, what was I feeling? Nostalgia for the White Christmases of my past? No. Anxious about how this precipitation might be messing up my future plans for this afternoon? No. Then I was candidate for being claimed by the Spirit of Christmas Present. I reached for my boots, the only uncertainty being whether to make a snow angel first or throw snowballs at the mailbox. As I opened the door to crunch out into God's virgin world, I remembered a cartoon of frazzled Christmas shoppers trudging wearily through the snow. In their midst was an enchanted child catching snowflakes on her tongue. Let her be our Saint of Christmas Present, as reminder that God is being born anew in each present.

21. CHRISTMAS FUTURE

The sad and guilty clutch of the Ghost of Christmas Past on Christmas present hinders some of us for readiness to encounter the "Ghost of Christmas Future." And yet, for others, the problem centers not so much on the depressing power of the past but even more on its impotence. Having somehow lost its ghost, Christmas has simply become boring. Attempting to prop up the power that Christmas we once experienced, we keep adding things. If the story of the Three Wise Men loses its allure, Van Dyck adds for us a story of the "other" Wise Man. Menotti provides the Magi with a side trip to visit Amahl. When the saint named Nicholas began feeling tediously pious, we gave him the secular oomph of being a fat and jolly chimney-slider. When his eight flying reindeer became so "yesterday," here comes Rudolph to the rescue. When even his shiny red nose becomes passé, just in time come Frosty, then the Grinch, and, yes, good old Charlie Brown. Yet such additions to inflate "meaning" into our tired Christmases are fleeting, for memory blended with fantasy yields sentimentality.

This ghostly anemia infecting a depleted Christmas Past is somewhat understandable. What's the big deal about an unwed mother so poor that she gives birth to her baby in the equivalent of a dumpster behind a Holiday Inn? This happens among street people all the time. What's the fuss about three foreigners making an unannounced visit, leaving a few Christmas presents, and departing "by another way," never to be heard from again? In fact, how did they get by Homeland Security? What's so special about birthing a child who himself falls out of sight for the next thirty years? And when he finally does show up, his tiny hometown disowns him. Then, in little more than a year, he gets himself into such trouble that he gets the death penalty. To make things worse, at his execution, even his so-called friends desert him. And finally, even though a few remaining groupies claim to have occasionally spotted him for the next few weeks, what difference does that make? The bottom line is that we are left in the same mess as we were when he was born. And while they gave him nicknames such as "Savior" and "Prince of Peace," our world is still laced with wars, violence, poverty, greed, and graft. So if Christmas future is no different from Christmas past and Christmas present, the hassled clerk at Walmart had it right about Christmas. "Let's get it over with as soon as we can."

But Christmas meaning can deeply reemerge when the Ghosts of Christmas Past and Christmas Present are confronted by the Ghost of Christmas Future—renamed the "Holy Spirit." The future becomes open-ended when the primal rhythm of life is forged by God's holistic Christmas action—as promise, as foretaste, and as consummation. What God did for us in the past identifies for us to see what he is doing among us in the present as a means of accomplishing his promise with us in an anticipated future. The one who came, is present, and is coming again. Faith in "what was" is the foundation for living the "what is" as foretaste of "what shall be." Christmas is about the conversion of memory into an enriched present marinated in a promise that births hope. The meaning of the season involves hyphenating all the three modes of Christmas, because any one without the others threatens to become toxic.

22. CHRISTMAS—A BAD IDEA?

It has taken the church a long time to figure out what to do with Christmas. For centuries it was never even observed. And when around the fourth century the church finally establish a calendar date for the birth of Jesus, it was arbitrary, likely chosen to compete with the pagan festival that observed the Winter Solstice. Even when in the Middle Ages a year was finally set for the time of Jesus' birth, it has turned out to be wrong by at least four years. To top this off, the Puritans became so incensed by the way that Christmas Day was being observed that any persons caught celebrating Christmas were put in stocks. Even to say "Merry Christmas" resulted in being fined.

With such a history, perhaps Christmas was a bad idea after all. Maybe we should have let the pagans have this date in the first place, today suing to have removed every sign daring to mention Christmas. Then secular America can have the day all to itself, celebrating an untainted "Happy Holidays" as an annual buying spree in honor of free enterprise. That way Christians could be punishable by disdain if caught on the day after

II. LIVING THE SEASONS

Christmas participating in the frenzy of Christmas present exchanging, the skirmishes for post-Christmas bargains, and the return lines for broken merchandise and negotiated refunds. In fact, by interviewing some of that crowd about their "reason for the season," we could likely conclude that "Christmas" had already been returned to the pagans.

Yet, what if we started all over again by gathering a remnant of Christians with a longing to reclaim the astonishing radicalness of Christmas? It would mean revising society's maxim that Christmas is for children by acclaiming that it is about being a child for the childlike. Our fantasizing would transcend sugar plum fairies into nothing less than the envisaging of a new heaven and earth. The cherished Christmas reading would come from Isaiah, prophesying a child named Immanuel who would be God with us (Isa 7:14 RSV). As a harbinger of hope, the promise is that he would birth within each of us an inner child capable of dreaming big time—fantasizing that "the wolf shall live with the lamb, the leopard shall lie down with the kid, the calf and the lion and the fatling together." Together we could have our own little Christmas parade in which this "little child shall lead them" (Isa 11:6 RSV). Born for the sake of this transformed future, "his name shall be called the "Prince of Peace" (Isa 9:6 RSV)

Admission into our Christmas celebration would be reserved for those prepared to wager that the day will come when "they shall beat their swords into plowshares, and their spears into pruning hooks; nation shall not lift up sword against nation, neither shall they learn war any more" (Isa 2:4 RSV). Forget the jolly red fat man stuff, and let the parade belong to the waving child, like the one whom Jesus placed "in the midst of them," and let her banner read, "Unless you turn and become like children you will never enter the kingdom of heaven" (Matt 18:2–3 RSV).

In the face of a society intent on providing abundant evidence to the contrary, let Christmas be for the remnant—those willing to live a Christmas Eve-type gambling on this vision so radical that only the childlike dare believe it. Advent yearning is for a Christmas hope that "the sufferings of this present time are not worth comparing with the glory about to be revealed to us. For the creation waits with eager longing . . . [to] be set free from its bondage to decay and obtain the glorious liberty of the children of God" (Rom 8:18–21 RSV). So if Christmas is our participation in God's gift-wrapped dream of creation's completion, then Christmas isn't such a bad idea after all.

23. CHRISTMAS LOVE AFFAIR

The church has never been sure what to do with one particular book of the Bible— the one named "Song of Songs" or "Song of Solomon." When some of us boys discovered it by chance in Sunday School, we took on a rapid and unexpected interest in Bible study. "I am sick with love," she pants, for "you have ravished my heart," "your kisses like the best wine"(Song 2:5, 4:9, 7:9 RSV). What an incredible contrast this is to the bored emptiness of life portrayed in Ecclesiastes, the book that just precedes it. Instead of all being "vanity and a striving after wind," we have a world of flowers, fragrance, radiant stars, a place where "the time of singing has come, and the voice of the turtledove is heard in our land" (Song 2:12 NRSV). Exciting. But why should this passionate love affair of two starry-eyed youth be part of the Holy Bible? Jewish scholars try their hand at justification by seeing it as symbolic of God's love affair with his chosen people. Paul sees it as reflecting the marriage between Christ and his church. And mystics such as John of the Cross see it as characterizing the Holy Spirit in love with our souls. But what if we build upon our previous suggestion of Mary's love affair with God the Holy Spirit? The scriptural portrait is of Mary as a mere teenager running off to visit her auntie, who is likewise pregnant by the Spirit's doings. Together they do their "girlie thing," probably with giggling slumber parties, for they are madly in love with the God who is in love with them.

What a contrast such poetic imagery of God is to the one Michelangelo painted on the Sistine Chapel ceiling. There, in the middle of everything, we see a Grandfather Creator who has not birthed an infant but has asexually created Adam as a grown man. Gone is the intimacy, for their fingers do not even touch. The entire ceiling portrays a cosmos vigorously male, overflowing with bulging masculinity, squeezing aside anything that might suggest youthfulness, femininity, tenderness—the joy of loving.

What if we permit the Song of Songs to provide our Christmas imagery for God—likening him to a gazelle running up and down mountains, wildly and crazily in love, rapping on windows, trying doors, writing love letters, gift-wrapping every portion of creation as Christmas gifts for us, his beloved! No wonder that when Mary greeted Elizabeth the child in her womb leaped for joy. With such a portrait, Scripture is rendered a marvelous love story—about the Lover God and we his beloved creation. One of Paul Simon's best songs is entitled "Crazy After All These Years." That's what Christmas is about—the poetry of a crazy love affair between a teenage

Mary and a teenage God, continuing to adopt us as an expanding family for trimming the cosmic Christmas tree.

24. CHRISTMAS AS ALWAYS

Matthew and Luke are the Gospels that have equipped us with our sentimental Christmas trimmings—amazed shepherds, warbling angels, munificent wise men, and a sweetly gentle baby in a stable illumined by stars. Nice touches, and yet with the stroke of a pen, John's gospel pushes aside all such garnishes and gets right to the point. From the very first verse he insists that this apparently illegitimate child, destined for failure as a crucified criminal, is very God of very God. So there! John proclaims that the Christmas event is nothing less than a genuine incarnation—the incognito of a fleshly God. Paul is likewise adamant that this fussy child with dirty diapers and annoying colic is the one through whom the whole cosmos was created, in a process of love following Love for the sake of love (Col 1:15–20 RSV). Such proclamations are staggering—declaring that the Christmas event discloses the extraordinary nature of God himself. "Whoever has seen me has seen the Father" (John 14:09 NRSV). Jesus distills the very character of God, the very soul of the divine, the very personality of the Almighty. Now that is revelation!

Thus Christmas is not really about a gifted child born to teach us how to be good. It is about a God who so plunges himself into our daily living that he takes our tragedies and betrayals into his own crucifixion. This means that Jesus Christ is far more than a thirty-year guest appearance by God—who shows up, only to return from whence he came, unchanged from his earthly stopover. If the incarnation is truly a disclosure of God's very nature, this means that God was, is, and forever will be the incarnate God in our midst. Throughout Scripture, we hear the cry for God to tell us his name. From Christmas Day on, we know it. Jesus Christ *is* God's name, and that name means Emmanuel—"God *with* us." For the Christian, shattered forever should be any image or even suggestion that God is distant, removed, or absent. Rather, the Christ event is God's marriage to humanity in a divorce-proof covenant—when after a thirty-year courtship, as it were, the consummation of this divine-human wedding occurs at Calvary, when Jesus as humanity gives himself totally to the Lover God. We stumble over words but somehow in the empty tomb we receive our adoption papers as born-again children of this marriage, rendering us brothers and sisters of one another.

In fact, the Eucharist can be pictured as a liturgical reenactment of this divine-human marriage. In this event we renew our wedding promises: that "until the end of time" God will be our wedded partner. Then by taking the body of Christ into ourselves, the Christmas incarnation is consummated—for "it is no longer I who live but Christ who lives in me" (Gal 2:20 RSV). At the altar/table, the family of God is rebonded as the fleshly body of Christ. In the Eucharistic Prayer for Reconciliation we hear, "You have bound the human family to yourself, through Jesus your Son, our Redeemer, with a new bond of love so tight that it can never be undone" (*The Roman Missal*, p. 760).

How appropriate it is, then, that on Christmas Eve Catholics have traditionally had their midnight Mass, and Protestants increasingly celebrate Holy Communion. Amidst the crèche and its angelic embellishments, it is really we who become the "Wise Men" as we bring our gifts of bread and wine. But in so doing, it turns out that we become the gifted ones, for by reaching out to receive, our hands become the manger for the ongoing birthing of Christ. And once we "ate and were satisfied," how could it be otherwise that we too will depart "by another way" (Matt 14:20, 2:12 RSV)?

25. CHRISTMAS AS BIG ENOUGH TO BE SMALL

Even though we intellectually know better, we have shared how much the portrait of God that loiters in our minds is the one resembling Michelangelo's painting—a grandfather wrapped in a mantle, like old folks need for extra warmth. If challenged, we acknowledge that God doesn't look like that—or look like anything, in fact. The invisible God has no ears, no nose, no face, no nothing, so that it is utterly impossible to picture God in *any* way. Yet this physical image tends to persist, pushing us to locate God spatially in some sort of "heaven," glibly referring to "the man upstairs."

Adventuresome satellites and Hubble telescope pictures have helped dispel such God-imaging, and yet, in all truth, this catharsis has been a bit disconcerting for us Christians. What is left really when there is no long a physical heaven above the clouds, no throne anywhere among the stars, no physical deity looking down over a parapet to engineer a miracle or two? We are left without a "where." Ours is a time when much of what we thought we

II. LIVING THE SEASONS

knew has been blown wide open, leaving us a bewildering cosmos beyond anything that previous centuries could ever have imagined. Many of our basic Christian writings were written during a time tenaciously holding to a flat earth divinely centered at the middle of everything. But we are now bequeathed a round earth that is simply a dot in a universe that is billions of years old, expanding outwardly into an infinite space of a hundred billion galaxies across three hundred billion billion light years—sweeping totally clean any possible physical God, or singing angels, or a populated heaven somewhere. With eviction of our Grandfather God from the cosmos, skeptics have an abundance of new data for jeering at the psalmists and at us: "Where is your God?" (Ps 42:10 RSV).

Yet, ironically, we Christians have reason to celebrate this emerging state of affairs. Even if we have not yet acknowledged it, we are being theologically purified of many of our unimaginative images of God. It is now possible for us to hear in a new way and with added emphasis what the best theologians have always insisted—that since God is mystery, any "god" who can be conceived is by definition not God. Instead, their best "descriptions" of God were in terms of who and what God is not. I would like to believe that they would welcome our Hubble age—theologians immersed in infinite space without edges, limitless time without ending, begun by an unimaginable "big bang" from an inconceivable dot of infinitely implausible energy. With such an astounding array of mystery, what better time than ours for speaking of a God without limits, who is everywhere but nowhere, whose domain is eternity but immersed in time, and whose center and circumference are identical?

Isaiah's poetic power provided prescience for this modern world—as he reaches for a God who precedes both light and darkness, creates well-being and delivers woe, designs the earth and governs it with wisdom and power, showers it with justice and peace, and gives vindication by bathing even us humans in glory (Isa 45:6–25 RSV). But it is Paul who pushes the poetry of our imagining to the edge. God is not a "being" at all, and thus is not a "somebody" needing to be placed somewhere, treated like an object that either exists or doesn't. As our efforts in locating God *within* the cosmos become bankrupt, our imaginations are lured into envisioning the cosmos as existing *within* God. In him we "live and move and have our being" (Acts 17:28 RSV). Space is the interiority of God's mind.

Relevant is the Christian belief that God creates "ex nihilo," from nothing. Analogously we can do the same, creating things in our mind by "taking thought." Thus we can envisage an apple that exists as long as we sustain it in our mind. So might be the mind of God, imagining and sustaining the cosmos by taking thought. God thought things into being, "and it was so" (Gen 1:9 RSV). Thus God does not hide from us; it is simply that it is impossible for us to get outside of God in order to "see" God. Instead, since God holds us in being, God cannot be doubted without doubting our own existence. Thus the question of "where" God is becomes as meaningless as any thought of God's "absence."

While scientists once worked within the limits of what was called verifiable facts, astrophysicists today are breaking open our imaginations in wildly fantasizing infinite universes of alternative dimensions, parallel worlds, string theories, and circular space. In effect, science has turned toward poetry, and in that sense, unknowingly toward theology. And we Christians, in turn, can turn into reclaiming the Mystery that is central to our faith.

Swept by the grandeur of such a portraiture, the incredibleness of Christmas becomes focused. John also acknowledged that no one can see God, but what if the invisible and unknowable one has chosen to make himself visible so as to become known on our terms? The eternal outside time has entered time, the Infinite has become finite, the God without limits has become limited, and the God beyond conceiving has become humanly conceivable. God has become knowable in an ordinary child with a bothersome cowlick. Such craziness is akin to the craziness we best know as falling in love. The God who cannot be seen has gifted us with an enfleshed self-portrait—signed in blood.

Amazing, but the question that immediately arises is, what evidence is there on which to gamble that this Jesus event is God's autobiography? John the Baptist sent his own disciples to ask this same question: "Are you the One, or shall we look for another?" (Luke 7:19 RSV). And the concrete evidence Jesus provided remains basic: do the blind see, the lame walk, the deaf hear; and are the lepers cleansed, and the poor given good news? In fact, Jesus later insists that the hungry, thirsty, naked, sick, and imprisoned are literally God's incognito. By interacting with "the least of these who are members of my family, you [do] it to me (Matt 25:40 NRSV). What good news indeed if these are the defining marks of God's character, and thus the anatomy of what God is about in the world.

Now there is one further step. Dom Helder Camara wisely observed that, for better or worse, the only gospel that most persons will ever encounter is that which is being lived by Christians. Therefore the primal evidence on which the world can gamble, one way or the other, on Jesus as the disclosure of God is how we Christians are living that faith. Evangelism occurs when in seeing us, people are sufficiently intrigued to ask, "Is this really what God is like?" What better time than in the midst of Christmastide for each of us to ask: "In looking at the character of my life, what do people really see?" How fine if they see hints of God's Christmas gift for the world.

26. IRONIES OF CHRISTMAS

Christmas is over so quickly. The very next day clerks busily return stores to "normal," leaving only half-priced Christmas cards and leftover wrapping paper. In contrast, as we have affirmed, the church officially sets aside twelve days for Christmas savoring. Sounds good, but a surprise awaits when the very next day after Christmas the church calendar commemorates Stephen as the first martyr. As if this is not enough to sober our Christmas mood, the next day marks the martyrdom of John the beloved disciple. Then, as if to make absolutely sure that we understand the cost of taking Christ's birth seriously, on the following day we grieve Herod's massacre of Jewish males two years of age or younger. How painful for Mary when Jesus must have asked why there were no boys for him to have as playmates.

While this way of observing the first full week of Christmas might be surprising, it shouldn't be. The cost of discipleship is a theme replicated throughout Scripture. This is distilled with particular power in how two of the greatest Old Testament heroes ended their lives. Moses's day of death was an Advent one, on the far edge of longing. Dying all alone on Mount Nebo, permitted only to see from afar the promised land to which he had been leading God's people for forty long years. Likewise David is forbidden to build as his final gift a temple fit for the God he had served all his life, permitted only to gather the materials with which another would build. Christmas never really came to either of them. Or perhaps better stated, both men lived the irony of Christmas as an IOU. Yes, but not yet. Now, but as a promise.

So primed, we are ready to explore the ironies of Christmas. The light shined in the darkness, yet the darkness continues its threat to overwhelm it. The angels sang gloriously of peace, yet there is more violence in the world today than ever before. In Christ all things were made new, yet day after day everything continues much the same. Christ earned forgiveness for us all, yet we continue to act like sinners. God came in Christ, yet we still await his coming. Christ overcame death, yet it continues to stalk the earth. Golgotha was once and for all, yet disease daily turns countless persons into grotesque crucifixes. And so Pascal seems right, that any religion that does not affirm God as hidden is a sham. Christmas helps us recognize how fragile is our precious faith. The good news strikes the ear of the world with the force of a hint, an innuendo from a manger, a wagering upon an angel song heard only by shepherds known for telling tall tales. Not even if snow adorns our Christmas Eve caroling do we have any direct, indisputable experience of God.

Instead, faith involves wagering on the Christmas ironies—in blatant contrast to our society, it means to trust the moments of strange peace dotting the landscape of our Advent hungerings; to discover ourselves more desirous of giving gifts than of receiving them; in being startled by finding ourselves preferring to be last rather than to play the game of winners and losers; when the apparent absence of God touches our thirst deeper than the presence of everything else. Christmas dawns in our Advent deserts when we find ourselves serving a God whom we do not see, loving a God whose love for which we can only hope, praising the wisdom of a God whom we do not understand, and thanking a God who in the Advent darkness can threaten to take away from us everything but the longing. The result? In the end it is the only Christmas gift we need—for "faith is the assurance of things hoped for" (Heb 11:1 RSV).

27. TENSES OF CHRISTMAS

My normal way of preparing sermons is to search the day's lectionary readings to discern a theme that can connect them. Yet the Scriptures for the first Sunday of Christmastide baffled me. Not only did there seem to be no uniting focus, but not one of the readings was in any way "Christmasy." Instead, they triggered a nightmare memory of walking into one of my PhD examinations with cold anxiety, sure that they would ask me the worst question I could think of. They did. "Trace the concept of time in all major philosophers from Plato to the present." Suddenly I realized that these post-Christmas readings were asking the very same question—the enigma of time. I passed the exam by knowing what other thinkers thought, but I would likely have failed if the exam had asked what I thought.

II. LIVING THE SEASONS

And here I was, forced by the deadline of a homily to avoid that question no longer. A hymn came to mind, the one about time being like an ever rolling stream that bears all who breathe away. "They fly forgotten, as a dream dies at the opening day." How dismal. Surely after the Christmas excitement, I could find more to say than that after childhood, life is downhill all the way. Rereading the assigned Scriptures from the perspective of time, the issue of tense arose. "How beautiful on the mountain are [present] the feet who brings . . ." (Isa 52:7 RSV). "All the ends of the earth will [future] behold . . ." (Isa 52:10 NAB). "O Sing [present] to the Lord a new song, for he has [past] done marvelous things" (Ps 98:1 RSV). Likewise, the reading from Hebrews contained all three tenses—"has," "is," and "shall be." The Gospel of John concurred, with the words of "was," "are," and "is coming."

I began realizing how abundantly we Christians are wrapped in this rich coat of varied tenses. Furthermore, I suggested that each stage of our life seems focused by a different tense. Our youth is characterized by future time, infecting us with an eagerness for what is "not yet"—for a puppy, entering grade school, a bike, cell phone, driver's license, dating, college, marriage, first job. The motivation for our youthful doings is a hope-wrapped future. Even for weeks before Christmas, "I can't wait" is our youthful mantra. Time cannot go fast enough.

Somewhere along our pilgrimage, time begins reversing until there comes a point of no return—a point that for some is a "midlife crisis." For me it occurred around my fiftieth birthday, when I realized that the time ahead had severely shrunk. The "rolling stream" of years had borne away far more years that any vigorous ones that might remain. We begin to feel as if we are backing into the future, or glancing increasingly through a rearview mirror as the dreams threaten to be only a "was." Christmas letters received from friends begin lamenting "how fast time flies." Their recurring mantra is "it seems like only yesterday that . . . ." They and I grumble about how busy we seem to be, as if sensing the need to cram more and more into a diminishing future of less and less. Then the mantra shifts a bit, increasingly becoming more urgent—"before it is too late." Instead of time moving too slowly, our inner pleading is for it to slow down.

My homily then gave thanks as well for being blessed by entering a third relationship with time. During my first visit to a monastery, I witnessed a strange exchange. Two monks were discussing what year it was, consulting a third monk. "I say it is 1971; he says 1972. Which is it?" "Isn't it 1973?" How unreal. Yet I now find myself at times consulting my watch regarding whether today is Thursday or Friday. While this could be a sign of Alzheimer's, hopefully it evidences living in a third kind of time—the anxiety-free kind that Jesus taught, analogous to the time mode of birds and lilies (Luke 12:22f RSV). With the troublesome episodes of our past purged of their "what ifs," and our future "if onlys" subdued by realism, we can enter thankfully into the consummate stage of "lived time," gifted with the deep fullness of each matchless "now." Intent on drinking each day to the cup's bottom, we are no longer tempted to taint it with what was or what might have been, nor gamble it away on ever retreating "maybes."

This Christian lifestyle of "Time Now" is analogous to what some theologians regard as God's time. For God there is no before or after, for God experiences everything as an ongoing present. For us to live that way would mean that each dawn births a Christmas Day, as the "once and for all" becomes a recurrent Present. The smallest of churches become Bethlehem, and in the tiniest crèche of the loneliest of nursing homes is where Christ continues to be born. And bread and wine lifted at millions of altars/tables is where Golgotha happens, as the world's sorrows and tragedies are elevated into Christ's cruciform redeeming of time. And as each person is reborn, resurrection happens.

Best of all, this third kind of time can flow back as foretaste in redeeming all stages of our time. It is all about now/now/NOW, in what Paul calls the "fullness of time" (Gal 4:4 NRSV). So let us raise a chalice with a concluding "Merry Christmas and Happy New Year," toasting all the moments of time that have ever been, standing on tip-toe at the edge of each fresh "now," in foretaste of every moment that can ever be. Why not, for everywhere the incarnate God is continuing to be born.

28. FINAL CHRISTMAS WITH THANKS

Many of us were brought up on a rigorous Christianity of demands and requirements, instructed to walk a path narrowly circumscribed by an overabundance of "no's." This working arrangement was overseen by a God with an enormous record book for documenting every slip-up—the one who was legendary for his quick temper, and ingenious in his assortment of punishments. The lifestyle that resulted tended to be painted the grey color of submissiveness, conformity, legalism, and insecurity, lit from a distance by a slippery promise of heavenly reward.

II. LIVING THE SEASONS

But I came to question whether Christianity so understood was much more than a religious version of the lifestyle that motivates nonreligious folk. The church down the road had a sign reading, "Getting to heaven is all that matters." The only real difference might just be the playing field on which one chooses to "make it big." In either case, the game of life was conjugated by these three verb forms: "to want," "to do," and "to have." Early on, I began feeling that something was hollow about trying to earn my parents' "love" by doing whatever they wanted, because the real dilemma was my inability to love the self that they seemed intent on molding their way. By hiding my real self from them, I was actually hiding myself from me. Although I did not realize it then, what was missing was the Christian verb form: "to be."

Everything began changing when I was discovered by an alternative version of Christianity—one that had little to do with negative living now in order to earn compensatory rewards in an afterlife. It highlighted a positive lifestyle *now*, one so self-authenticating that there was no thought of "reward" later—or at all. The joy of living as an authentic Christian is its own compensation, needing nothing more than itself. What was being ignited in me was touching the deep longing to be formed into the unique, irreplaceable, and beloved self that God had created me, and each of us, to be. What delight there would be in being freed from the frantic obsession to "become someone," to "make something" of one's self. Dislodged would be the driving obsession to be the center of everything. One would be loosened, freed, by having punctured the craving for recognition and compensation. "I," "me," and "mine" would no longer be the pronouns of choice for determining value. They would be replaced by "we," "yours," and "our."

But for this to happen, healing is indispensable—nothing less than conversion. Significantly, the epistle readings for Christmastide are from the First Letter of John. He puts things straight—the one "who does not love does not know God; for God is love" (1 John 4:8). God and love are a hyphenated pair, as cause is to effect, binding our knowing to our being. What had been missing in my Christian formation as a child was this God-love connection. Love had not been even remotely what I felt toward a demanding and punishing God. John is so very right in insisting that the real change needed can happen only when we are loved, for to be loved is the defining craving in each of us. Only then is it possible for us to become loving, as we are being loved. Otherwise we remain demanding love-empty selves who are unlovable because we are full of ourselves. We are trapped, for every effort to gain love by making ourselves lovable is motivated in a preoccupation to make ourselves the obnoxious center of everything. We are inevitably curved in upon ourselves, and the gyrations of cosmetic appeal are lethal.

But not only does St. John's letter make our dilemma clear, but he provides the Christian way for our dead end to be reversed. "We love because he *first* loved us" (1 John 4:19 RSV). Since every effort at earning love is of necessity motivated by self-love, this can be reversed only through the gift of God's undeserved love for us—not because of anything we have done but in spite of it. Our dilemma, residing in seeking to be loved, can be healed through the transforming gift of realizing that we are already loved.

This is the Christmas gift that "keeps on giving." Amazing is the way in which it transposes us from the drive to "get" into the passion to "give," expressing to others the love that we are graciously receiving. Our possessive drivenness and envious clutchings are undone at the root. The childlike beauty called Christmas, then, is all about this silent surgical work. Divine love is the Christmas gift that so takes us by surprise that we are turned inside out. God's love, distilled as a helpless Christ child, discloses the amazing vulnerability of this love—given without conditions, extended without gimmicks, presented without strings—offered so completely that there is simply no need of promised rebates. Being embraced by God's love is all that we could ever want, rendering our living into a loving "thank you."

Therefore before we pack away our crèche and undress the tree for another year, let's take one final look at Christmas to be sure that we've "got it." God loves us in the adoring way that Mary gazes upon her beloved child. Therefore the gauge for how well we are appropriating this mangered love is the degree to which we find ourselves no longer obsessed with competing, getting, controlling, and winning. Instead, the gentle gratitude of being divinely loved bequeaths in us a Teflon soul, becoming immune to the external hurts and intimidations that can tempt us from "giving" to a defensive "getting." Thus the dictum to "love your neighbor as yourself" is best understood this way—to "love your neighbor as you are being loved," which is through Christ. Blessed are those who are humbled by the surprise of such love, for they know themselves to be on God's permanent Christmas card list.

II. LIVING THE SEASONS

29. NEW YEAR'S, JESUS, AND THE CALL

Christians seem edgy about books and movies that depict Jesus as being human. We seem more comfortable with a Jesus who is all-knowing, all capable, all-certain—all divine. Yet this is to deny the heart of the gospel. God's defining act is in becoming incarnate in the human Jesus, identifying completely with our plight, becoming totally like us in all things but sin. The book of Hebrews goes all the way by insisting that Jesus "in every respect has been tempted as we are" (Heb 4:15 RSV). For forty days and nights he underwent an ordeal of tempting, with Satan continuing to appear to Jesus "at opportune moments," right up to his crucified fear that God might have abandoned him. Being human has to do with the little things as well, for he caught colds, teased girls, and played games. His knowledge was limited, insisting that "no one knows the time . . ." (Matt 34:26 RSV). He declared that he was not perfect, for no one is perfect but your father in heaven (Mark 10:18 RSV). He evidenced terror, sweating drops of blood at the prospect of being crucified, "and began to be greatly distressed and troubled" (Mark 14:33 RSV).

We should not be surprised, then, that Jesus never clearly declared himself to be the Messiah. Doubtlessly other Jewish boys of his time pondered if they were called to be the one for whom the Jewish nation was yearning. But the decision as to who would be the Messiah was totally God's decision. Thus it would have been arrogant, even presumptuous, for Jesus to have declared himself Messiah, no matter how strong his inklings. Instead, he modeled for all of us the life of the Christian as one of self-emptying, of becoming open to be guided by God in each moment—wherever that might lead and whomever that would lead him to be. God has a unique "calling" for each one of us, and our defining task is to be led into that tailor-made vocation. "The lot marked out for me is my delight" (Ps 16:6 Grail). Therefore Jesus was lured forward, as we too were, into his calling, learning from his mistakes, as he "increased in wisdom and in years, and in divine and human favor" (Luke 2:52 NRSV). For thirty years he was gently being led, his conscience forged by immersion with the poor, his sensitivities honed as a simple village carpenter, his responsibilities shaped by dutifully supporting his widowed mother and siblings, his mind profiled by pondering and praying alone in walking the morning and evening hills.

One day he heard that his cousin John was being drawn into the calling of prophet. He felt led to see for himself—and upon arriving at the river bank, he was drawn into the water to be baptized. It turned out that John was the one who discerned that it was Jesus and not himself who might be being led toward messiahship. Perhaps, but immediately the Spirit led Jesus into a heavy desert testing of such a calling, for well over a month. On the one hand, there was the temptation simply to walk away from all such "nonsense," content to marry a lovely Jewish lass and raise a family in a quiet Jerusalem suburb. And, on the other, was the temptation to force God's hand into performing some miracle so that Jesus could be certain—such as turning stones into bread, as was Satan's suggestion. It was in refusing both kinds of temptation that Jesus had his courageous breakthrough. He emerged from the desert experience with greater clarity and determination that he must let God lead, step by step, wherever this might lead, even to crucifixion. So this is how our lives are to be led—in total openness to whatever, never knowing with certainty the when, where, what, or often why. Moment by moment, we are to be open toward a future we do not define, trusting a God who opens and closes doors, sensitive to hunches that challenge logic, and favoring imagination over realism. The final words of Jesus distilled not only how he died, but how he lived. "Not what I want, but what you want" (Mark 14:36 NRSV).

With Jesus as our model, then, we too are to live mindfully the goadings and lurings of the "hound of heaven," discovering that unless we let ourselves be led into our singular calling, we will never find rest. Discipleship means "to follow," wanting nothing more that to be who God desires us to be, content only in doing whatever pleases him. Therefore it is appropriate on New Year's Eve or Day to begin the New Year by making a promise to live our lives in this fashion. In the thirteenth century, Saint Dominic provided us with a classic prayer for this Christian posture. "Take Lord, and receive, all my liberty, my memory, my understanding, and my entire will, all that I have and possess. You have given it all to me; I now give it back to You, O Lord. All of it is yours now, dispose of it according to your will; give me only your love and your grace[;] that is enough for me." In 1755, John Wesley composed a comparable promise for Methodists to make each New Year's Eve. "I am no longer my own, but thine. Put me to what thou wilt, rank me with whom thou wilt; put me to doing, put me to suffering; let me be employed for thee or laid aside for thee, exalted for thee or brought low for thee; let me be full, let me be empty; let me have all things, let me have nothing; I freely and heartily yield all things to thy pleasure and disposal" (*The Book of Worship*, The Methodist Publishing House, 1952, p. 52–53).

II. LIVING THE SEASONS

Making such a "renewal of covenant" testifies to what Jesus learned on our behalf—that when the road of our pilgrimage "diverges in the woods," the Spirit's tendency is to draw us toward "the path less taken." As we move this week toward Epiphany, let us recognize the wisdom of the Wise Men,"who followed a star that no one else saw.

30. EPIPHANY WISDOM

Unfortunately for many women, Christmas ends with a sink full of dirty dishes, as the males in the family fade into an afternoon nap. Yet Christmas is not supposed to end until Epiphany, which is twelve days later. Only then is the Christmas tree to come down and the carols quieted. This extended Christmastide is not necessarily because Christians enjoy partying, but because it is intended to be the "boot camp" for our retraining—rehearsing the Christmas rhythm so as to make it second nature within us. Thus refreshed and reequipped, we are prepared to enter "Ordinary Time" faithfully.

While the four weeks of Advent shaped our taste for anticipation and hope, the ten days of Christmas are to lavish us with sensitivity to the richness of life as gifted. And now our retraining reaches Epiphany—meaning "to make manifest," as the Magi did in taking the good news back with them from whence they came. So just as we "contaminate" our Advent longings by singing Christmas carols prematurely, and just as we abort our Christmases by limiting them to one day, so here we muddle the meaning of Epiphany by placing the Wise Men figures at the crèche alongside the shepherds. But their appearance as marking the threshold into Epiphany is to happen twelve days after the Christmas Eve sheep-tenders heard the angels and returned to their pondering (on what thus is also called the "Twelfth Night"). And the theme of Epiphany comes as still another surprise—that in giving we receive far more than we gave. The Magi came with gifts, and returned gifted. So it has been ever since, that when we bring the gifts of bread and wine to the manger-altar, we return transfigured. Joy comes from sharing a good news that is too good to keep. And so it was with the Wise Men, returning "to their own country by another way." That follows, for once we encounter the Christ, we can never return the way we came.

The week of Epiphany is intent on reforming us so that whatever we touch becomes "epiphaneous." Symbolically the candles taken down from the Christmas tree are not for storage but for dispersal—placed not under a bushel basket but on the tallest lamp stand, as a buoyant glow for a darkening world. Appropriately, the final day of our Epiphany training ends the following Sunday with the baptism of Jesus, serving as a powerful reminder that our own baptism was our initial epiphany. And the confirmation that followed was our commitment to the Holy Spirit's claim of squatter's rights on our lives. With or without camels, we are readied to enter Ordinary Time as "wise ones," obedient to the Epiphany crescendo culminating the Gospel of Matthew. "Go therefore and make disciples of all nations, baptizing them in the name of the Father, Son, and Holy Spirit, teaching them to observe all that I have commanded you; and lo, I am with you always, to the very end." Happy New Year!

31. BAPTISM—HIS AND OURS

The Advent-Christmas-Epiphany season officially ends with the Baptism of Jesus on the first Sunday after Epiphany. At first glance, it seems odd for the church to celebrate the baptism of the adult Jesus only twelve days after the Wise Men came to celebrate his birth. Yet there is wisdom in disregarding for a moment the thirty intervening years, linking these two events together with the theme of birth and rebirth. They remind us that just as our physical birth involved being drawn from the water of the womb, so our spiritual birth occurs in being drawn from the water of the baptistery.

Parents who inquire of clergy why they should have their child baptized are often fed anemic answers, and sometimes downright strange ones. Their questions need to be taken seriously. What meaning is there in sprinkling an apparently innocent child as if she were unclean? And if one waits until adulthood, how much different is that from secular rites for joining a lodge? By linking the two births of Jesus, the manifold meanings of baptism begin emerging. At Christmas, Jesus was born fully human as Mary's son; at his baptism, he was declared fully divine as promise that through our baptism we are adopted by "sonship" into the family of God. Jesus was born in the embrace of a Virgin Mother; at his baptism and ours we are embraced by the one disclosed as our Father. Born with the Holy Spirit as his father, Jesus' baptism promises the Holy Spirit as our incarnate companion. At his birth, the divine became human; at his baptism our humanity is being made divine. At his birth, he came from eternity into this world as his home; at baptism "the heavens were opened" as promise of our homecoming. Jesus was baptized not to be made holy by water, but to make the water holy by which we are baptized into newness of life. The Spirit of

II. LIVING THE SEASONS

God descended like a dove at his baptism, promising us a dove-like descent when confirmation becomes our Pentecost.

The Old Testament provides baptismal imagery as well. God led Israel toward the promised land with a cloud by day and fire by night; in Christ's baptism, the cloud dissipated, disclosing that it is the Holy Spirit who leads by fire to our promised home. Passing through the waters of the Red Sea, Israel became God's people; in Christ's baptism, God himself entered the waters to rebirth us as his church. At our Red Seas, the incarnate God does not tell us to go ahead, but plunges in himself to lead the way. Instead of walking "dry-shod" between "walls of water," in baptism we are engulfed by that water—so cleansed of our burdens that it is with a lilt in our steps that we can take the desert road less taken. And as in baptism the seeds of Jesus' calling were watered, so in our baptism God's purpose for each of us is seeded for the nurturing. Therefore birth for the Christian is for the sake of rebirth; and because Christ underwent it first, following him into dying and rising is not so much frightening as downright exciting.

32. CANDLEMAS BY CANDLELIGHT

As we shall keep discovering, forty is one of Scripture's favorite numbers. Since the resurrected Christ is portrayed as remaining with his disciples for forty days of final missional preparation, the church decided long ago that forty days after Christ's birth would be a symbolically appropriate day for celebrating what it called Candlemas. It was a Jewish practice for a mother to be purified by offering a sacrifice in the temple after the birth of her child. (Lev 12:1–12 RSV). In addition, the first-born child was to be "redeemed" by being "consecrated to God," recalling how the firstborn of the Egyptians was sacrificed for the liberation of Israel (Exod 13:2, 13 RSV). And so it was, ironically, that Mary and Joseph "redeemed" Jesus, the one who was to redeem all of God's people. Their sacrifice was the one prescribed for the poor who could not afford a lamb. So, ironically again, Simeon recognized this Christ child as himself the lamb to be sacrificed as "a light for revelation" to the world (Luke 2:32 RSV). Appropriately, then, the church gave this commemoration the name "Candlemas."

There is something special about candles. Even persons with no religious sensitivity are softened by a candlelit meal; and even cynics are inclined to pause at the sight of floating candles on a pond at a rally for peace. We Christians, in turn, adorn our altars with candlelight, and mystics become spiritually mesmerized by contemplating a candle flame. My own imagination is whetted by thoughts of what a Christmas tree full of lit candles must have been like for our grandparents. Thus it makes sense that the church through the centuries has celebrated with candles this dedication of God's firstborn Son as "the light of the World"—the one whose death lit the way from here to eternity.

Early on, this Christ-lighting event became further enriched by having Christians bring to church a supply of candles to bless for use in their homes throughout the new year. Then at twilight daily each family would bring one of the candles to Vespers, light it from the perpetual Christ candle, and return it to provide light for their home that night. This practice became even more deeply nuanced during a period in Ireland when Catholics were suppressed. Because priests were forced to celebrate the Eucharist in secret, a candle was placed in the window of the chosen home to guide the faithful to the event, for what was truly a candle-mass. Somehow related is the continuing practice of lighting a candle for safety during a severe storm.

How fine if we Christians were to restore some of this rich tradition. How simple it would be, for example, if in each home the evening meal would begin with a candlemas lighting of a candle, symbolizing the "eucharistic" awareness of Christ's promise to "eat with you, and you with me" (Rev 3:20 NRSV). After the meal, the candle could be placed in a window, where all night each Christian home would be an hospitable witness to the one whose "light shines in the darkness, and the darkness has not overcome it" (John 1:5 RSV).

33. MEETING JESUS AGAIN AND AGAIN FOR THE FIRST TIME

When the infant Jesus was brought for dedication in the temple, someone special was awaiting him—Simeon by name. He represents us in our own Advent waiting, for in a deep sense neither he nor we dare to "see death" until we behold Jesus (Luke 2:25 RSV). Like my niece who waited "all her life" to meet Mickey Mouse, so we like Simeon have waited much of our lives to meet the one for whom all humanity is secretly yearning. Only when this happens can we whisper with Simeon, "Now you are dismissing your servant in peace . . ." (Luke 2:29 NRSV). Meeting Jesus for the first time brings a peace that not even death can shatter, no matter how many times it may threaten.

II. LIVING THE SEASONS

But this doesn't mean that after this meeting everything will be to our liking. Not at all, for Simeon recognized in this child "the downfall and rise of many." Actually it may take a number of Advent-like falls before the meeting happens. Mary is our model, for of her Simeon predicted a heart-piercing sadness—as many folks know with their own children. Life is a serious business, so that even in the midnight glow of a Christmas tree "the inner thoughts of many will be revealed"—to our shame (Luke 2:35 NRSV).

Advent has to do with our deepest yearning. Christmas is the name for its intersecting with Jesus for the first time—in such a way that we can "depart in peace" trusting that it will not be the last time. In seeing Christ as the "salvation which thou has prepared in the presence of all peoples" (Luke 2:31 RSV), Simeon could die—believing in the one who in dying would bring rebirth, who in plaguing us would bring healing, who in threatening us would enact forgiveness, and who in blinding us with light would render us light-bearers.

Since our baptism is into "the light of the world," many churches give a candle to the person being baptized, which is to be used. No matter how lonely we might become, no matter how depressing things may weigh upon us, it is in lighting the baptismal candle that we can be reclaimed by that tranquility that Simeon was given—a peace at soul depth without which it can be fearful to be, at any time. But in having it within easy reach, we are met again by God's ongoing promise: "I'll leave the light on for you."

34. LOST AND FOUND

Having been refashioned by the "high" of our Advent-Christmas-Epiphany triad, we are readied to enter into the gray, cold sameness of winter's Ordinary Time. The prospect of such bleakness should make of particular interest the Scriptures that the lectionary provides for our transition. They begin with a graphic portrait of Hannah aching to be a mother, feeling deeply the emptiness of her sterility (1 Sam 1:9–20 RSV). Desperate, she goes to the temple, only for her prayerful entreaties to become so emotionally distraught that the priest chastises her for being drunk. In the accompanying New Testament reading, a man is so possessed by an unclean spirit that he screams out with insane rage in the synagogue where Jesus is teaching: Jesus of Nazareth, "have you come to destroy us?" (Mark 1:24 RSV).

These readings hardly seem designed to provide a supportive threshold into Ordinary Time. Yet upon closer examination, this sterile woman and this desperate man both have a resemblance to us when we become overwhelmed by ordinariness. And what they disclose is the theme of God's favorite games—"Take Away, Before Giving," and "Lost and Found." I suspect they are alternative names for the same game.

How this plays out is that when Hannah's hopes are totally dashed, when there is nothing left to do but to throw herself utterly into the arms of God, that is when she becomes what she was no longer is able to dream—a mother. But there is more. This miracle of the *empty hands* is completed only when in receiving all that her heart desires, she no longer clutches, but returns the newborn child to God—where at the temple he becomes one of the great prophets. Similarly, when the deranged man shrieks in desperation his recognition of Jesus as "the Holy One of God," only then does he become what he never dared to dream—sane. And here, too, the empty hands miracle is completed only when in receiving his heart's desire, he does not clutch it to himself. Too good to keep, he becomes an instrument whereby this message about Jesus is "spread everywhere throughout all the surrounding region of Galilee" (Mark 1:28 RSV).

It is during Ordinary Time that we stand best able to understand the degree to which these two stories of transformation are not rare. They are simply examples of the healing that results from God's finest playing of his game of games. As the jaws of death engulf Jesus, when he can only cry out his "why?" to God in the despair of failure, only then does the impossible possibility happen. Death's gates are shattered in resurrection. The bleeding cross of brokenness becomes the empty cross of hope. And here again, the miracle of the empty hands now pieced is completed only when he, and we, do not clutch the good news to ourselves, but go excitedly to "make disciples of all nations" (Matt 28:19 RSV).

Alcoholism, depression, unfaithfulness, imprisonment, sterility, nightmares, impotence, betrayals, death—these are the ingredients haunting our Ordinary Time into numbing "ordinariness." And the miracle part? It occurs daily—in the realization that these "failings" are at the top of the impossible list about which Jesus insists: "With God all things are possible." Thus our two scriptural stories turn out to be quite timely after all. It is during Ordinary Time that we are most tempted by our stifling ordinariness to "beat up on ourselves," tempted to go back down the alligator paths of our past hurts and failures—to be bitten yet another time. But on some

II. LIVING THE SEASONS

overwhelmingly ordinary day, immobilized by the tedious, dreary, insipid, monotonous, weariness of our ordinariness, the miracle of the empty hands can occur. Too drained to go down any path anymore anywhere—that is when in giving up, we can receive all that matters. In having so little left, that is when we can come to experience ourselves as actually quite blessed, simply in being alive. Halted in our pretense of being somebody we aren't, that is when the awakening occurs—to find that we are someone.

The illusion of living when we are actually only existing, that is the experience of sinning against hope. Ordinariness becomes oppressively ordinary when "it all depends on me," caught in the lonely struggle to disguise my ordinariness. But when "burn out" strips us of our feigning, that is when the Spirit is able to blow into flame a yearning for something deeper than the boredom of sameness. Somewhere between the void and a rigid wall, there occurs on the reverse side of our spiritual bankruptcy a signature in blood, signing off as paid in full the liabilities impounding our living for so long. What then follows is a miraculous peace simply in being ordinary. Trusting that with God the impossible is impossibly possible, whatever might actually happen no longer matters. "Now" is sufficient unto itself, realizing that the object of God's game is to win by losing, with the prize being the gift of relinquishment—able with Jesus to utter to our last whisper, "Into your hands I commit my spirit" (Luke 23:46 RSV).

The psalm that the lectionary provides for this transition into Ordinary Time is the ironic mantra for "losers." "My heart exalts in the Lord. I rejoice in my victory." Relinquishing to God the ordinary self that we barely had, that is when our winning is a second birthing into a childlike enchantment, for all things once "ordinary" have taken on an uncommon sacredness. May we be blessed with living such ordinariness for a long, long time.

35. MARDI GRAS AS A BOOKEND

Mardi Gras marks the last day of Ordinary Time, the day before Lent's forty-day "sacrificial rigor" that begins tomorrow, on Ash Wednesday. There are cities where this event has become an elaborate final fling into a libertine bacchanal, complete with masks to hide the identity of those who would not otherwise dare such desecration of the original meaning. Mardi Gras means "Fat Tuesday," so named because the ingredients used in rich fried cooking are to be used up before beginning our Lenten blandness.

For the same reason, this day has also been bequeathed the name "Pancake Tuesday," a delightful way of ending our frying.

But the original meaning of this event was that it completed a three-day observance called Shrovetide, which with the Triduum (the three days of Maundy Thursday, Good Friday, and Holy Saturday) serve as Lent's two bookends. "Shrove" is the time for "shriving," meaning "to write down" as a personal confession those thing for which one then receives forgiveness.

Yet if we "shrove" *before* Lent, what is Lent for? In spite of a widespread misunderstanding, Lent is not intended to be a time of denial by which to earn forgiveness. Rather, it is our shroving that grants us forgiveness, with Lent being our *response* to having been forgiven. Christian healing is a process that involves five steps: contrition (being sorry), confession (concrete admission of sins), forgiveness (received as a free unmerited gift of God's love), satisfaction or "penance" (undoing as much as possible the damage one has done), and reconciliation (living ongoingly the consequences of this healing process). The misunderstanding concerning Lent centers in the word "penance," which can suggest a punishment that one must endure in order to earn forgiveness. Instead, a better word is "reparation," meaning to repair situations for which through forgiveness one is now able to take responsibility. So understood, our Lenten actions are to be positive rather than negative, done in grateful thanks as a healing response for being healed.

To illustrate how this works, after hearing the confession of a husband's undeserved anger toward his wife, after granting absolution a priest should not assign him a negative penalty, as if in punishment. Rather, a wise priest might propose that the confessee take home a rose to his wife, or take her to a special restaurant. Effective "reparation" would involve a reconciling token of his love. So understood, we need to reinterpret the idea of "Lenten sacrifices." If one chooses to "give up" chocolate cake, the rationale should not be as a negative self-reprimand but as a positive first step toward a healthier diet.

Shrovetide, then, should be our first mindful step in the time-honored process of Christian healing. During these three days preceding Lent, we might well make an inventory of our lives, writing down as confession our commissions and omissions, and then praying for God's concrete forgiveness. So prepared, we can enter Ash Wednesday as humbled but forgiven repentants, beginning Lent with a dual focus. The first is to take responsibility for the effects of our forgiven angers, insensitivities, and alienations,

II. LIVING THE SEASONS

working at undoing as much of the damage as possible. The second is to filter our living by promising a concrete disciplining—thereby lessening our propensity to act out of a recognized weakness. What better way to anticipate Easter than in aiming for a changed lifestyle surmising resurrection.

36. ASH WEDNESDAY AS A WALDEN POND

Ash Wednesday is the day traditionally set aside for inward fasting, marked outwardly by an ashen cross on one's forehead. It is a day to remind us of Henry Thoreau's reason for "going apart" by building a cabin on Walden Pond. Acknowledging that most folks live quietly desperate lives, he did not wish to die without having lived. Thus he took an Ash-Wednesday-year to "take thought," reflecting on life's meaning —until he would be able to live each day intentionally. His friend Emerson provided the benediction for this venture: "What a waste is the unexamined life." To exist is not to live.

Ash Wednesdays provide such a pond. And while they officially come yearly, they more often come unannounced. They might happen the day we are forced to place an aging parent in a nursing home; or when a nurse calls us about the test results indicating urgency in seeing the doctor. Life goes around only once, and, sooner or later, each of us gets assigned the "night shift." Ash Wednesdays are those times when we are brought to wonder if the brass ring for which we have been frantically reaching may actually be made of plastic. These are the violent moments that expose our deepest motivations. "I do it for me!" "To be seen!" Ash Wednesday might come when from a shadowed corner a voice weirdly whispers something about how the left hand shouldn't know what one's right one is up to. Rocking on Thoreau's front porch, one ponders about how good one would actually be if there were neither pay offs nor punishments.

The six-week adventure from Ash Wednesday to Easter is the space specially set aside for pilgrimaging from a self-centered living for me toward a God-centered living for others. It can be a humbling climb, for the measure of our progress is unambiguous. Are we able to act authentically even if no one is watching what we do, will never find our what we have done, or care one way or another about what we might accomplish?

There is more. Ash Wednesdays are to extend beyond personal accountability. The biblical prophets insist as well on social accountability. Each of us is not a solitary island, but more like an archipelago. Isaiah's words spoken 2,700 years ago are as timely now as when he was resolute about his nation "taking thought." The "fast" that God chooses for you, Isaiah insisted, is "to share your bread with the hungry, and bring the homeless poor into your house; when you see the naked, to cover him . . ." (Isa 58:7 RSV). Lenten restitution involves not only "me" but "us." We are to be responsible in working for release of those unjustly imprisoned, untying the yoke of sweat shops, providing low-income housing for the homeless, seeking employment for the marginal, sharing our nation's affluence with a starving world, and turning exorbitant weapon expenditures into resources for building a world that is "like a watered garden, like a spring whose water never fails" (Isa 58:11 RSV). Lent is for Easter.

"Remember that you are dust, and to dust you will return." These are the humbling words of Ash Wednesday. Elvis's rendition is, "You're nothing but a hound dog." T. S. Eliot's slightly more sophisticated version is that God "will show you fear in a handful of dust." Only persons marked by dirt have a clue as what to yearn for behind the closed door at the top of the stairs, whose staircase is being built by the Lent of our Ash Wednesdays.

37. ASH WEDNESDAY AS COMPLINE

Monks are intent on living literally Jesus' teaching that God hands out time only one day at a time. If the Vigil bell breaks the night's darkness for us, we awake to receive the resurrection gift of one more day. Our spontaneous words are "Christ is risen; he is risen indeed." After worship with its silent pondering, at daybreak the bell calls us to Lauds (meaning "praise") in order to chant with joy our full thanksgiving for the Christmas gift of this unique day, unlike any other in all of history. Our day is divided into three-hour (Trinitarian) segments involving personal prayer, spiritual reading, and work. Each begins with corporate worship as our way of rehearsing Christ's incarnational intersections into our time, chanting from the one hundred and fifty psalms that were his own hymn book. The day's closing segment is appropriately named Compline (meaning "complete"). It is when we return this day that we have borrowed from God, hopefully with interest.

In summer, Compline enfolds the church in brilliant sunlight; in winter the exchange is in total darkness. Whichever the dance rhythm, it is our daily Ash Wednesday, preparing us for the "death" of relinquishing the only day we have. Compline begins with a silent review of our day, having been verbally reminded not to let the sun go down on our anger. "First be reconciled to your brother" (Matt 5:24 RSV). Each person needs a Compline

II. LIVING THE SEASONS

in order to end the day with cleansing honesty—asking who should I have called to say "I'm sorry" and who should have heard me whisper "I love you." The Compline encounter can be simply stated: "If this were truly my final night, what still needs to be done for me to have "a restful night and a peaceful death"?

Then we come forward to the altar to be sprinkled with the water of reminder—enabling us to stare into the face of death in the knowledge that through baptism we were so immersed into Christ's death that our death has been died for us. Wrapped in this resurrection pledge, we have the courage to walk the long corridor into the deathlike "Great Silence." Each monk lies down on his bed, and surrenders his life as did Jesus: "Into you hands, Lord, I commend my spirit."

There will likely be a tomorrow, but it is not at all certain that I will be part of it. For those tempted to live otherwise, Jesus has a parable. It is about a person planning a tomorrow by tearing down his barns so that he can build larger ones that will guarantee a future of eating, drinking, and being merry. The name Jesus gives to such persons is direct. "You fool, this night your life will be demanded of you" (Luke 12:20 NAB). Our daily Ash Wednesday is intent on rebirthing the humility of knowing that none of us are more than "a mist that appears for a little time and then vanishes" (Jas 4:14 RSV). God deals out life's cards one at a time—in order that by "taking no thought of the morrow" we are enabled to live every second of today to its fullness.

The forty evenings of Lent may provide each of us with multiple Complines with which to discern those phone calls, emails, letters, visits, and acts needed in order to make our peace with God, friends, strangers, enemies, and ourselves. As a child I eagerly marked off on a calendar the days remaining until Christmas. A Lenten equivalent might be an Ash Wednesday list of things needing reconciliation, with check marks indicating the proximity of Easter.

38. LENTEN CHOICES

Lent is about choosing. Moses put before Israel, and us, the choice of choices: "I have set before you life and death, blessing and curse; therefore choose life . . ." (Deut 30:19 RSV). Folks today tend to avoid either/or choices, preferring the both/and type. Yet we actually make an enormous number of either/or choices daily. In most other countries, the choices are narrower, as, for example, between white bread or brown, cola or ginger ale. In contrast, our supermarkets inundate us with choosing from thirty kinds of cheeses and twenty-five brands of cola—each pre-weighted by multimillion-dollar advertising hypes. In fact, such choices are no longer even limited to store hours, for at 2 AM one can send a decision by laptop from one's bed.

Lent involves facing this situation head on. Advertising brazenly insists that in choosing Dr. Pepper "there is nothing more that I need want." Such mini-offers trivialize the meaning of choice until we can almost believe that "the Hokey-Pokey is what it's all about." A culture deluged by inconsequential choices is inclined to blind us to the deeper issues of life that cry out for consequential choice. Lives are frittered away that do not render intentional decisions regarding the what, how, and, above all, the why of it all.

Ash Wednesday marks the powerful yearly posing of Moses's either/or question. But once the decision is made, three ironies begin emerging. First, Christian living requires that the choice be remade daily. Jesus insists upon it, that "those who would come after me" must "take up his cross daily and follow me." Human decisions are thin, so that *daily* we must choose, mindfully. Temptations erupt daily, and so the ongoing call for decision—whether to lose our lives by being sucked back into society's competitive consumerism, or by give our lives away to God and thus for others (Luke 9:23–25 RSV). A choice "to gain the whole world" means forfeiting one's authentic self, while the Christian style of losing means gaining in a deeply contrasting sense. Choose.

The second irony is that persons who do not make the choice are permitting the decision be made for them, usually by society. While this has a strange parallel to the Christian, it is with a totally different meaning. In making the Christian choice, the meaning of life that is birthed is so amazing that it could not really have been the result of one's own choosing. We have been chosen—given a gift we did not deserve. What really happened was that Lent's choiceful questioning backed us against a hard place, until the false self experienced itself as impotent even of giving itself away. It is in being chosen that we are made capable of choosing the choice. So the Lenten decision, in the end, is who shall we permit to choose for us—society or God.

The third irony is that the meaning of Lent emerges most powerfully not when we succeed in our Lenten promises but when we fail—chocolate cake and all. When Jesus confronted his disciples with what discipleship would actually involve for them, they exclaimed hopelessly, "Then who can be saved?" Jesus' answer says it all: "For mortals it is impossible, but not for God" (Mark 10:23–27 NRSV). Ash Wednesday, then, is a time for choice-making; Lent is a time for testing the choice; and Easter is a time for realizing who actually enabled the choice to be chosen.

39. SOCIETAL REWARDS AS CHRISTIAN SIN

The church is quite talented in takings the apparent randomness of our living and shaping it scripturally into meaningful patterns worthy of celebration. The number forty that characterizes the days of Lent is a symbolically rich example. Noah's flood to renew the earth lasted for forty days. Moses lived in Pharaoh's court for forty years; evoking a fleeing into forty years of sheep-tending formation; as preparation for freeing God's people by leading them to Mount Sinai where for forty days he received the Ten Commandments as foundation for forty desert years of disciplining as preparation for entering the promised land. Jonah enabled the redemption of Nineveh by prophesying its destruction in forty days. Saul was king for forty years, followed by David, who ruled for forty years. Elijah fled for forty days as preparation for hearing God as the still small voice. Jesus had forty days of desert temptation as strengthening for bringing all the forties into redemptive culmination. There were forty days between the transfiguration and Good Friday.

Lent, in turn, is our own forty-day pilgrimage through the forties of God's pilgrimage with his people through forty hours in the tomb to the consummation that is Easter. What is evoked is an awareness that our baptism is a participation in God's redemptive flooding through Noah; our fasting is one with Moses's fasting in preparation for receiving on Sinai the redemptive Word; our wandering is one with Israel's desert years. Our own fears participate in those of Elijah in fleeing for his life; and our ongoing temptations parallel those of Jesus who was like us in every way but succumbing. No wonder the color of Lent is violet, its music negligible, its Ash Wednesday and five Friday fastings are mini-Good Fridays. Marriages are to be postponed, parties frowned upon, and the word "alleluia" discouraged from even being whispered. Lent is serious business—a time of decrease as the necessary "means" for increase.

Yet if the "means" are permitted to become the "end," they are no longer Christian. "Lent," meaning "spring," has a hopeful intent. Thus while Lent has a negative flavor, it is never intended to be the primal seasoning for the whole of Christian living. Lent is a season and not a perpetual state in which to remain. To confuse the two is deadly. It is to be preparatory, a hopeful cutting away of underbrush on the Easter path toward joy.

Yet our Easters, in turn, should never be permitted to swallow up our Lents. Both form the rhythmically upward pattern of Christian living. It is indicative that Jesus's forty-day desert temptations did not culminate in his Easter-like baptism, but the opposite. His baptism came first, followed by his period of intense temptations. Consequently, baptism as our own Easter immersion is not the culmination that ends our temptations. It is the event that intensifies them, beyond anything that our nonreligious neighbors can imagine. St. Paul wisely shared his own experience that before learning about God's law, he was without sin. Sin occurs after learning about the good, for it is in "knowing better" that we are left without excuse. Our Lents, then, are preparations for our Easters; and our Easters are preparations for our Lents, each in turn spiraling us into purer levels of faith and existence.

This pattern of escalating levels is well illumined by the three kinds of desert temptations that Jesus endured. Together they expose how difficult it is to be a serious Christian in our increasingly secular culture—for while these three temptations are at the heart of the Christian understanding of sin, they form the backbone of society's game plan for success. What society promises as rewards for conformity, Christians understand as seductive lures into inauthenticity. What society regards as laudatory behavior, serves for the Christian as models of failure.

To illustrate, the first temptation facing Jesus was *power*. While his version was the lure to turn stone into bread, today's equivalent might be Viagra's power for self-adulatory sexual prowess, yearning for the four-hour side effect. Or it might be the coveting of a luxury sports car throbbing with needless horsepower. Or an obsession with Sunday afternoon's football violence. Power is the desire for having things my way, or else. Go team!

Jesus' second temptation dealt with *possessions*. Our economic system thrives on instilling in each of us a craving to "have it all, now!" Enough is never enough, not even more upon more! "Be patriotic, go shopping." Society's economic "health" is measured by the interplay of a growing "consumer confidence" with an expanding "gross national product." The stock market's daily gamblings are regarded as an indispensable ingredient of the evening "news." "Making it big" is the bottom line. "Play Lotto and Win it All."

The third temptation is *prestige*, attempting to lure Jesus into participating in a TV spectacle of doing a swan dive from "the pinnacle of the temple" to the cheers of adoring crowds—and the ten o'clock news. Modern prestige depends on appearance—on where one is seen and with whom, cosmetically choreographed by the media to match the latest styles. How seductive is the temptation to give away everything for fifteen minutes in the spotlight. Expose tabloids at every checkout counter tempt us to envy the hottest fleeting sensation, and to gloat over the glitzy rumors of the latest "fallen." *American Idol* is appropriately named.

In contrast, the holiness that Jesus taught is of a "wholeness" that contests radically our culture's portraiture of the "good life." He modeled a cheek-turning vulnerability rather than competitive power; nonviolent forgiveness instead of ego aggression; and second-mile vulnerability replacing instant vindication. His way is that of peace rather than contention, community rather than individualism, sharing rather than accumulating, humility rather than prestige, and friendship that refuses to let anyone be an enemy. Through the eyes of Christians, "depraved" is the appropriate name for society's darlings who trample each other in a mad scramble for the transient "temple" pinnacle. Lent involves our ongoing recognition that the dynamics of society's acclaimed functioning are temptations into hollowness, on a path to a good Friday that has no Easter.

40. THE WALL, LENT, AND PASSING THE PEACE

I was not prepared for the impact of the Vietnam Wall. I could hardly find it, for unlike the pretentious monuments overpowering Washington, this one is almost invisible, largely submerged beneath the ground. It begins as a walkway gently descending. Step by step it feels as if I am becoming my country, drawn downward into what we did not expect and increasingly did not want. The wall becomes higher, expansively so, until it is over my head. I am becoming engulfed as a participant. There are only a few names with dates at the beginning, but relentlessly the dead keep piling up, by months, then years—engraved so as to scar my own body as they glare back at me from the polished black marble surface.

REASONS FOR THE SEASONS

When I begin walking, I feel alone, but each step brings an increase of strangers. One woman is tracing a name with her finger. A child is placing a doll for her father at the base. Parents are holding hands. War buddies embrace each other as the point. A man in fatigues cries as he shakes hands with a former hippie protester still wearing his long hair and beads. A couple tries to explain the inexplicable to their infant son. This is holy ground—where the ambiguities of judgment, repentance, and reconciliation are intertwining, somewhere on the far side of ideology.

Since that experience, I have fantasized about adding to this special place. What if we constructed a twin wall on the right side of the walkway, and on it engrave the parallel names and dates of the Vietnamese who died. The two walls would begin fairly far apart, as if at a hostile distance; but during the descent they would begin approaching each other. At the deepest point they would touch, as if in a stalemate, an impasse. Yet there would be an opening at the bottom through which persons could pass—one at a time, and only for those willing to do so with bowed head. Upon passing through, one would find on the other side that the names on the two walls are reversed, as if confounding who is aggressor and who is defender. Repentance means "reversal," as in a re-remembered past. The walkway would continue ascending, as it does now, turning us free into an open field.

A key task for the Christian, harder than asking for forgiveness from those whom we have hurt, is to forgive those whom we have experienced as hurting us. It may seem like a small thing for someone to say "I'm sorry," but it is huge. It entails courage to take responsibility for what happened, no matter what for us the "facts" may seem to be. These are the attempts at selflessness that can "rekindle the gift of God"—disclosing that "God did not give us a spirit of cowardice, but rather a spirit of power and of love and of self-discipline" (2 Tim 1:7 NRSV).

This fantasy of reconstructing the wall might have a parallel in the symbolic act of passing the peace during Communion. Never intended to be either a polite nod or a bone-crunching friendliness, it is the indispensable response to Jesus' therapeutic teaching. "So when you are offering your gift at the altar, if you remember that your brother or sister has something against you, leave your gift there before the altar and go; first be reconciled to your brother or sister, and then come and offer your gift" (Matt 5:23–24 NRSV). Jesus is referring not only to the things that we have done, but also to those "second mile" things of asking forgiveness for what may not have

II. LIVING THE SEASONS

been my fault. Communion is the peace forthcoming from treating others as Christ is treating us.

Sometimes one hears the complaint that passing the peace takes too long. Perhaps, but if it happens as intended, probably not long enough. What if during one of the Sunday services during Lent we actually provided sufficient time to do it well? Every congregation has some folks who are not at peace with each other, some who avoid certain others, some who harbor secret grudges, some who refuse to speak to each other, and some of us who do not care enough to learn the name of strangers. This expanded time for passing the peace could lure us to find a person to whom we need to say, "Please forgive me when . . ." or "I don't think I ever said how much I appreciate you," or "we need to find time to do lunch together." Faith empowers us to face walls of all kind, and thereby render them opportunities for love to find a way through. After half an hour of passing the peace, the pastor might reassemble the Lenten congregation with Jesus' words: "You are not far from the kingdom of God" (Mark 12:34 RSV).

41. LENTEN DISCIPLINE AS JOY

Sometimes Jesus can be downright confusing. Take for example his insistence that not only did he not come to abolish the law, but "whoever breaks one of the least of these commandments, and teaches others to do the same, will be called least in the kingdom of heaven" (Matt 5:19 NRSV). Yet the scribes and Pharisees had ample occasions in which to chastise Jesus and his disciples for not following the law, as in hand-washing and observing the Sabbath. Further perplexing, this same Gospel of Matthew has as its intent to portray Jesus as the new Moses providing new laws, so that the Ten Commandments of Mt. Sinai are supplanted by Jesus on the Mount of the Beatitudes. Paul seems to go the whole way by insisting that in Jesus the old covenant of the law is abolished, replaced by a new covenant of grace. This ambiguity crescendoed into an attempted resolution when at the Jerusalem Conference the early church concluded that Gentiles do not have to become Jews, thereby dispensing the law totally as being a "yoke upon the neck" (Acts 15:10 RSV).

No wonder, then, that confusion can reemerge during Lent when the traditional Lenten disciplines of "giving up" are treated as if reinstating some of the law's legalistic "thou shall nots." One clue in finding our way through this apparent muddle is in understanding that Christ's "making all things new" refers not so much to the "what" as to the "why." The syntax of the law is "*Do* in order to receive," rendering obedience the means of acquiring. The Christian syntax, however, is reversed: "*Because* you have received, now you are freed to do . . . ." The effect of Jesus' life, death, and resurrection is the unearned and undeserved gift that frees us to become whole. In spite of our spotty success in keeping any rules, there persists deeply within each of us a yearning for the impossible—to hear God whisper, "You shall be called 'My Delight'" (Isa 62:4 NAB). Amazing grace is that Jesus Christ whispers just that—with a sizable megaphone for those with faulty hearing aids.

Therefore Christian living is not about what we "must" do—either to receive a reward or to avoid punishment. Once one begins hearing Christ's words of delight, we are remotivated with a joyous desire to please him. Fed by God's love, the "you shalls" are transformed into thankful "you mays." We are free to love by being loved. "Since God loved us so much, we also ought to love one another" (1 John 4:11 NRSV). Not really "must," but "may," by finding that we "can." Such a response to undeserved gifting is spontaneous, for by being freed from obedience to the letter of the law we are enabled to live gratefully the spirit of the law. Obedience to the letter, on the other hand, is a self-interested duty that makes us slaves to doing. But the response to love renders us free to be thankful children excited to please our Father.

How then can both be true—that Jesus does not remove the law, and yet things are totally changed? It is because "the love is the fulfillment of the law" (Rom 13:10 NAB). Thus may our Lenten disciplines no longer be motivated by the intent of giving up something in order to receive, but regarded as ways of relearning the why and the how of thankfulness.

42. POSITIVELY NEGATIVE AND NEGATIVELY POSITIVE

I confess that there was a period in my life when I hadn't a clue as to what to do with Lent. As a child, it was clear—that it was supposed to be a negative time of "giving up." No more Saturday afternoon cowboy movies, so forty days and nights without Gene Autry, Hop-Along Cassidy, Roy Rogers, and, of course, Trigger. And what this "giving up" taught me was that God was something of a sadist, and that with Christianity came a strong dose of masochism.

II. LIVING THE SEASONS

Vatican II was helpful in modifying my attitude, for it shifted the mood of Lent from negative to positive—proposing it not so much as a time for avoiding the bad as it was for doing the good. Yet if Lent only means trying a little harder to do what I am supposed to be doing all along, doesn't that make Lent pretty thin? It was finally in the Ash Wednesday liturgy itself that I came to recognize that both understandings are right—if the negative and positive are so hyphenated that they feed each other. The liturgy provides alternative wording to be used in administering ashes. "Remember, you are dust, and to dust you will return." These are words intent on extracting a humbling negative promise concerning what we intend *not* to do. "Turn away from sin and be faithful to the gospel." These are words intended to elicit a positive promise of what one intends *to* do. It is in pulling them apart as either/or choices that the dilemma occurs. They need to be regarded as inseparable, but with a proper order.

Crucifixion is for resurrection. The negative is for the positive. Scripture readings for the first Friday of Lent illustrate this both/and approach. Isaiah insists that the "negativity" of voluntary fasting is to be a "positive" way of identifying with those whose fasting is non-voluntary (Isa 58:1–9 RSV). The negative prepares us for the positive. Denial is what enables our doing—in releasing those unjustly bound, freeing the oppressed, feeding the hungry, sheltering the homeless, and clothing the naked. In Isaiah's understanding, this positive doing is not to be restricted to individuals. In fact, he calls for something a bit like a National Lenten Day of Fasting. And if Isaiah were invited as the White House speaker for such an event, he would "cry out full-throated and unsparingly aloud" against a nation of enormous disparity between the rich and the poor, the comfortably insured and those without health care, the college preparatory academies versus ghetto schools without textbooks, gated communities in contrast to cardboard shelters under bridges. After breakfast, Isaiah would distribute bumper stickers: "May Americans live simply, so that the rest of the world can simply live." The responsorial psalm for this White House day would serve as a hope wrapped in confession: "A humble and contrite heart O Lord you will not despise" (Ps 51:17 Grail). The event might be embarrassing, but how nicely rare that would be.

The New Testament reading for this first Friday of Lent provides a both/and version. When Jesus is asked why John's disciples fast but his do not, he declares that negativities such as fasting are not to be ends in themselves, but preparations for the "wedding feast" of Christ the "bridegroom"

(Matt 9:14–15 RSV). Our grocery store tabloids specialize in stories that slake our jealousy by inviting us to gape as persons who more and more get their "comeupance" by being brought to the less and less of obesity, divorce, or scandal. In contrast, the Bible as "tabloid" portrays those who in choosing less and less are blessed with more and more—of a different kind.

I remember some years ago when my Lenten promise was a rigorous determination to master contemplation. Evening after evening I fidgeted during my self-enforced thirty minutes. With clenched hands and tensely methodical breathing, I was hell-bent on "learning silence." Then one night, near Easter, I became totally fed up with the constant carnival going on in my head—and I just gave up. "I can't do it." Frustrated, I sat miserably as a violet replica of twilight failure. But quietly through an open window I began to be aware of a shyly gentle breeze hinting a spring freshness. In spite of myself, I found myself "letting go" and sinking into it. Less was becoming more; emptiness was becoming openness for filling. I still regard that timeless evening as a rare blessing. It was when the nothingness of silence was no longer soundless. This discipline of layered quietness was actually for the sake of mindful hearing—as wind through pine branches made music. The sound of a contented cow somewhere in the valley became a Vesper blessing upon the world. And the gentle giggle of a playing child bathed the evening with the innocence of Eden.

I know now that Lents are to be training grounds for using the negative in a positive way, living with less of assorted kinds so as to rebirth "mores" of a very different sort. Perhaps I understood more than I realized, because one Lent after enduring the five movie-less Saturdays without Roy Rogers, I used my saved nickels to treat two neighbor kids who couldn't afford it—to come with me after Easter to meet Trigger.

43. LENTEN FORGETTING THROUGH REMEMBRANCE

Isaiah is a favorite prophet of this season because he expresses well our Lenten hope—that God will "remember not the former things, nor consider the things of old." God's "new thing" is the promise to do just that. If God *forgets*, then "I will make a way in the wilderness and rivers in the desert" (Isa 43:19 NRSV). Yet while God's forgetting is our hope, Lent, ironically, must begin as a time for *remembering*—so that God, and thus we, will be able to forget. The mind of each of us is peopled by disturbing memories, and all of us struggle to shove the most painful of them out of sight into the nooks of our psychic attics. This rarely works, for without warning they can erupt to gnaw our days and growl at our midnights. None of us are without a history of such bruises—sad, ugly, and hurtful—both given and received. And when Lent begins by rubbing a few of them raw, that is when the Easter promise becomes an urgent yearning. If only it were true that "those who sow in tears shall reap in joy."

But how? The Lenten courage to rummage among these painful memories commences with a craving for peace—an internal peace, and an external one with our relationships. Especially fragile are the sensitive memories of childhood, when we were so vulnerable. They need to be touched carefully with soft gloves. As children we had to develop coping habits in order to survive—often by learning to respond in the way in which we were being treated. While such coping may have been palliative then, as we move into adulthood they continue to prompt our attitudes and actions in ways that are often counterproductive. Not only are we inclined to hurt others in ways that we have been hurt, but we remain overly sensitive where the deepest bruises continue to be soft. When our survival skills feel threatened, we exercise undue defensiveness. And the faults we so freely find in others are often those for which criticism has fallen most harshly on us in the past.

The contours of our present "shadow side," then, are mapped by the way stations of our woundedness. What others have done to us and what we have done to others—these ricochet off the walls of our present, with echoes of anxiety, anger, resentment, and guilt. This is why our Lenten promises to act different largely fail, for we cannot will to feel differently than we do. As a result, Lenten promises are often exercises in self-deception, in which the past remains a carousel, for we are incapable of forgetting.

The reason why Easter is so central in Christian living is that it marks the event in each of our lives when the burial clothes of our tomb-like past are laundered by the promise of the Divine forgetting, thereby becoming "cured memories." On the landing at the top of the forty Lenten stairs is a door marked "Good Friday." Lent entails detecting the cross-shaped nails poking around in our memories, those continuing to "get under our skin, and with which we are tempted to prick others. Reaching the top with at least one handful of the memory nails, we are gifted with a hammer. Redemption is a richly powerful word—meaning to buy back, pay off, re-establish, make up for, settle accounts. It involves recovering, satisfying, converting, fulfilling, releasing, restoring, delivering, sacrificing, ransoming, repossessing, pardoning, healing, and cleansing—and all of this occurs through the forgetfulness of God's forgiveness. The Good Friday door can be opened, but only by nailing onto it the scarred memories of our unhealed "bad Fridays."

Much of the pain of our childhood was in having to deal with the hurts by ourselves. But by nailing them onto the door of Christ's cross, they are no longer mine to deal with, but his to dispose. In contrast to the secular jibe to "shake it off," the Christian alternative is far more effective—to "offer it up." All of it. And with the final nail, the Good Friday door opens, its reverse side marked "Easter." The expansive space opened out in front of us is our "Pentecost"—the Holy Spirit's promise of ongoing companionship in selective forgetting.

The Isaiah Lenten passage with which we began expressed hope for the divine forgetfulness. After twenty-two chapters of ruminating over the past, the prophet is ready to hear the words of God, that his hope has become fact. The God who promises amnesty through amnesia has done just that, so that "the things of the past shall not be remembered or come to mind" (Isa 65:17 NAB). Thank you Jesus!

Yet there remains one further step, often the hardest—for *us* to forget. We are tempted to forget God's forgetting and thus acting as if it is we who must bear the burden of forgiving ourselves. As a result, we permit our damaged memories to remain like old computer files on "repeat," unable to find the "delete" key. Christ knows where it is, for it is one of his favorite ones. Yet our skeptical self-programmed computer will likely keep displaying the prompt: "Are you sure?" Really sure? But if just let it happen, the divine finger will gently guide our nervous one to the definitive "Yes" key. Then on the screen appears the invitation called "New." And when pressed, there will appear a "blank document" called Easter. It's all about fresh beginnings.

44. LENTEN INVENTORY

Significant change is not likely to happen unless each of us does an honest periodic inventory of who, what, where, and thus why we are. While one of our favorite social sports is pointing out the dumb mistakes and flaws in others, taking stock of one's own liabilities is an infrequent game of solitaire. Therefore it is wise to make Lent our yearly appointment for the exercise of candid mirror gazing. But one of the best mirrors is not a "selfie," but the eyes of an honest friend or two. Yet seeing one's self through their eyes rarely happens—nor they through ours. Because all of us shrink

II. LIVING THE SEASONS

from seeing ourselves as we truly are, our friendships have a dimension of dishonesty, rooted in an unspoken mutual agreement to edit carefully our verbal feedback. "I wouldn't want to hurt him" is a typical restraint. The result is a form of mutual blackmail in which those very persons who know us best are those least likely to tell us what we need to hear. In all honesty, a friend who might dare such honesty is not likely to remain a friend for long. The ideal would be the unlikely friendship that can actually function as a creative two-way mirror because the feedback is wrapped in a mutual love whose intent can be trusted. A surrogate would be a spiritual director. But, in the end, the only fully trustworthy mirror of eyes happens through a friendship with God.

But let me suggest two fairly reliable vehicles for providing objective data to our Lenten review—our checkbook and our schedule. Monthly we scrutinize our checking account in hopes that it financially balances; it needs to balance spiritually as well. So is with our schedule of activities. Helpful, then, is having mirrored back to us as a whole our year's expenditures and activities in terms of Jesus' criteria: testing our love of God in terms of time and resources spent in feeding the hungry, giving drink to the thirsty, clothing the naked, healing the sick, visiting the imprisoned, and welcoming the stranger (Matt 25:34–46 RSV). Basil the Great (fourth century) even goes so far as to suggest that one's house and garage can be objective mirrors of our living. He gets disturbingly concrete by suggesting a review of the surplus food in our pantries and freezers in light of the hungry. Likewise revealing are the unworn clothing and extra shoes in our closet in the light of the needy. He even insists that the unneeded money in our bank accounts and stock portfolios actually belong to the poor. "You do wrong to everyone you could help but fail to do so," he says. Standing before such mirrors as these, our self-perspective takes a significant shift. Our need for forgiveness falls heaviest not on what we have done as much as on what we have failed to do. Our failings are more in our omissions than our commissions.

These forty days for such a Lenten scrutiny do not include Sundays. These are our "days off," as it were, for every Sunday without exception is to be reserved exclusively for celebrating the resurrection. Even during Lent, then, they function as "little Easters" at the head of each week, reminding us that the Easter stone to be rolled away from our shadows is in order to free us to be stone-rollers for others. While these mirrors for measuring the "radical hospitality" of our lifestyle may seem a bit harsh, we will find in the eyes of those whom we help the deepest hints of resurrection.

45. LENT AS A BOTH/AND

For us cradle Christians, our Lents may have left us with an aftertaste. We tend to remember them negatively as times for giving up what we most liked. As a boy I coyly suggested giving up spinach, only to be informed categorically that it was not on the list. Apparently it had to hurt, like giving up ice cream. Early on I blamed Catholics for all this because their legendary Lenten disciplines were beginning to guilt-trip us as they previously relaxed Protestants, who had barely heard of Lent and certainly not of ashes.

Then about the time we Protestants were getting into the swing of things, Vatican II came along and lightened up on Lenten sacrifices, and focusing instead on Lent as a positive experience. One of the new Lenten prayers at mass even went so far as to pray, "Thank you Lord for this joyous season of Lent." Instead of the former focus on our weaknesses through self-denial, the tempering became an invitation to perform affirmative deeds of charity and mercy. Instead of guilt-tripping us into change, the "tactic" seemed to be more that of positive reinforcement. This Catholic mood shift could be sensed even in the modified approach toward death. Instead of a black-garbed priest doing a Requiem Mass with its frightful "Day of Wrath" for those facing judgment, there was now a white-vested priest who celebrated what was popularly called a "Mass of the Resurrection," complete with Easter hymns.

Yet sometimes correctives need correcting. If every day were a Thanksgiving, we would all become obese; and yet if there were no yearly Thanksgiving, we would likely take things for granted even more than we do. If every day were a Christmas, we would become spoiled brats; yet without it, life can tend to be just one doggone thing after another. If everyday were an Easter, we would have little compassion for the world's crucified—the poor, marginalized, suffering, and imprisoned; yet without it, we would tend to wallow in our "good Fridays" of depression and cynicism. Here again, a both/and approach seems creatively valid.

We see the either/or approach to our faith being questioned as well in contemporary efforts at restoring the meaning of the Eucharist. While Catholics formerly stressed the altar as an event of sacrifice, the Vatican II shift pulled the altar away from the wall in order to restore the idea of a table around which we gather in communion and fellowship. But Protestants, in turn, who have long insisted upon having a Communion table, began pushing the table against the front wall in order to restore the symbolism of an altar. And now the reform of the reform is suggesting a both/and approach, for to celebrate the Eucharistic fullness we need a table in symbolic foretaste of the heavenly banquet to be; but just as certainly we need the symbolization of an altar, for without Christ's sacrifice we are left living in a fantasy fellowship. Steak with attractive supermarket wrappings promises feasting, yet it shields us from the stark sacrificial truth that all living depends on something dying. Thus the importance of an "altar-table."

This both/and approach is an ecumenically reconciling call that applies to much of our faith. For example, the Protestant empty cross without a corpus can smack of sentimentality, yet with only the Catholic crucifix our joy can be smothered in dour duty. Celebrating death is an exercise in illusion, yet resurrection without crucifixion muffles the fragile preciousness of each moment of existence as gift. Comfortable Protestant sitting without kneeling can cloak the cost of discipleship, while excessive kneeling can suggest that Christ's yoke is not as "easy" as he maintained. We need each other.

So it is that there is wisdom in hyphenating Lent-Easter, for they marinate each other. This gives to Lent a negative-positive alternation in which there is a relinquishing and a receiving, a forgiveness and a forgiving, a remembering and a hoping, a discipline and a foretaste, a defeat and a victory—a time for spinach and for ice cream. A Lent-Easter can help keep us from domesticating the wildly sweeping lows and exhilarating highs of Christian living—for both are the reason for the season.

46. LENT AND THE POWER OF WORDS

Words have an incredible power. They can *hurt*. Three words screamed by a child are a body blow to any parent—"I hate you!" We all use words as weapons, holding our favorite ones in reserve for lashing out at an errant friend as with a malevolent hammer. But words can also bring *peace*—as in "it isn't malignant," "the jury finds you not guilty," "let's try again," and "Mom, I was wrong; I'm coming home." Words also have an amazing power to *create*. With only a few words, God created the cosmos. "Let there be light," and there it was. Words, too, have an enormous power to *redeem*, as when the Word becoming flesh incarnated three divine words: "I love you!"

The Lenten season is when the church specializes in three other words: "You are *forgiven*." It is almost beyond conceiving that a sordid page of our life can be erased, that our slate can be washed, that our dirty clothes can be laundered as "white as snow." Is this possible in today's throwaway world where things are no longer made to be restored, refurbished, or repaired, but discarded, trashed, and replaced? In a society such as ours where persons are treated as expendable numbers, it is hard to believe the Christian insistence that each person is precious, irreplaceable, and thus reparable.

The genius of Protestantism is in stressing the power of words in preaching, and such verbal power, in turn, permeates all of the church's life—as in the words of absolution, commendation of the dead, matrimonial binding, and eucharistic consecration. And as medical schools are beginning to realize the power of words in the healing process, so the church needs to regain in all its fullness the power of Lent's healing words. The *Consumer Reports* volume on "How to Clean Practically Anything" needs to be completed with a section on Lent. Billions of dollars are spent yearly on therapists who help in diagnosing the autobiography of the problem, but they cannot say the authoritative words of healing that the church offers for free: "Pick up your bed and walk; your sins are forgiven you." So powerful are these words of absolution that the Catholic Church regards them as a sacrament.

Concerning this forgiving authority bequeathed the church, Jesus makes a remarkable declaration: "Whatever you loose on earth shall be loosed in heaven" (Matt 16:20 RSV). That is why some early Christians postponed baptism until their deathbed, figuring that they could never again be as pure as at this baptismal moment of "total reversal." Protestant churches are beginning to appreciate this ongoing power of forgiveness more fully by establishing times and ways by which to "remember your baptism and be thankful." This power of the baptismal event as an act of confession and forgiveness needs to be offered ongoingly, with Lent being the most cherished season for doing this.

Forgiveness operates in two directions—toward what which we have done or failed to do, and toward that which has been done to us. All of us have scarred and been scarred—with a whole arsenal of put-downs, ridicule, abuse, abandonments, betrayals, jealousies, control tactics, and vendettas. That which we have been done and that which is being endured, they both have the power to damage us within and without. While they can both be lethal, they are both embraced within the healing power of forgiveness—but done in the right order. It is in receiving forgiveness that we are empowered to forgive.

However one handles such Lenten matters as chocolate cake and Diet Coke, let us spend time this Lent in identifying at least one of our active wound-memories. Then pray: "God, forgive them, for they may not have known what they were doing. And forgive me, for I probably did. Amen."

47. PALM SUNDAY AND THE LAST CHAPTER

Sometimes things actually do go well, especially in the spring. Flowers, graduations, weddings, gardening. And so with a dance step to a warm breeze, we can cross the threshold from Lent into Holy Week, leaving behind the wearying forty days—for this is Palm Sunday. "Bless is the One who comes in the name of the Lord." These are the happy words, sung easily along the triumphant parade route into Jerusalem, spreading our football jackets out on Route 66, lifting our palm branches and fishing poles as an archway. To have actually been there must have been a mountaintop experience. But you can't live there. Mountains are exhilarating in the climbing, but one must always climb back down into the same old sameness, carefully. So it is with our Palm Sundays. It doesn't take long for reality to grab us by the ring finger. In fact, many churches let us peak only for a few minutes of palm waving, and then plunge us into hearing the long rest of the Holy Week story. When read in parts, there is reserved for us the congregation the hateful words of the Palm Sunday crowd turned murderous: "Crucify him!" Even on Palm Sunday, we are forced, as Paul Harvey used to put it, to "hear the rest of the story."

And the rest of the story is what incriminates us: "All his acquaintances stood at a distance" (Luke 23:49 NAB). How quickly the dream dies, the hopes dilute, and the blame begins. It was only a month or so before this, for many it was only a week or two, when folks flocked to him from every village and region, so believing his every word that they trusted their loved ones into his healing hands. Utterly amazing was this man—then it all turned sour. The two heartbroken disciples walking to Emmaus drew the fatal conclusion: "We had hoped he was the one . . ." (Luke 24:21 RSV). But it is over now, all over. Palm branches dry up quickly, lilies turn a yucky brown. So on the morning after, we can't dodge the question: who really betrayed Jesus? Don't ask.

REASONS FOR THE SEASONS

Forty years ago there was a theological movement called "the death of God." Well, Good Friday is that event for every Christian. And Holy Week relentlessly leads us to it. That Friday was certainly not "good" in the living of it. And the worst day in human history was the day after—Holy Saturday, the living of which was hardly "holy." For us Christians, that day and a half should be a mandatory red-letter immersion in nothingness, hour by hour. One cannot have even a hint of an inkling of the difference that Easter makes unless we have undergone the intensity of a tragedy that strips us of every hope for any happy ending to anything. Only in somehow experiencing crucifixion first hand can resurrection have much more substance than a chocolate bunny. Yet it is impossible for us to walk realistically with those first disciples into their devastation. Why? Because we have read the whole story. We know how it will end. We have been told the "happy ending." But the disciples hadn't a clue. And on that fateful Saturday there was no way that they could take a sneak look at the final chapter. Only rain-drenching pathos.

I used to find it puzzling that after his crucifixion Jesus was unrecognizable to every one of his closest friends, from Mary Magdalene to the upper room disciples to the duo traveling to Emmaus. Every single one of them thought he was a total stranger. I think I am beginning to understand. We tend to see what we expect, and discount what we regard as unbelievable. His followers were so drained of all hope of ever seeing him again that they could not believe that which was before their very eyes. Our world is like those Good Friday disciples, watching either from afar, or crying with Mary at the foot of some cross. Either way, this crucifixion forces each of us to ask the question of questions: "Who is Jesus, really?" He poses decisively the enigma of our own finality. How we answer defines for each of us our destiny. If the answer we muster is that "he was a carpenter from Nazareth, a very good man"—that is bad news, really bad. The bottom line that follows is that good folks die young, while for the rest of us, it just takes a little longer. Yet if in staring at that grim spectacle we are able to behold the autographed portrait of God, then everything is turned upside down, inside out. That is good news, unbelievably good. That realization is our moment of resurrection—our encounter with a God whom we could never before have imagined, and otherwise would not have been able to recognize. Here is the suffering companion who agonizes with us, for us, and by us—the supreme lover whose love not even death can thwart. The death of

II. LIVING THE SEASONS

God turns out to be the dying of God in ongoing suffering for a crucifying world—and is overcoming.

Easter for the disciples, then, could in no way have been expected or predicted from within Holy Week. Yet Easter in no way undoes or even dilutes that week. Easter is the final chapter that flows back over the whole, transforming Palm Sunday, Good Friday, and Holy Saturday into a single plot entitled "The Greatest Love Story Ever Told."

48. UNCERTAINTY AND HAPPY ENDINGS

It is said of us Americans that we crave happy endings. It follows that our favorite movies are variations on the theme of boy meets girl, boy marries girl, and both of them live happily after. This is probably because life yearns for placating touches of fantasy—because way down deep we know better. Life just isn't like that. And yet, unwisely, we tend to act as if it were so. At the beginning of the twentieth century, a favorite societal slogan feels a bit astonishing today: "Every day in every way we are becoming better and better." "Progress" was the positive byword, and we even gave World War I a happy twist by heralding it as "the war to end all wars," ushering in "a world safe for democracy." While such fantasies have become smudged, they incredibly cling on as our working spectacles. Through them we behold the world as a B movie, harboring the assurance that in the end those who wear the white hats will defeat those wearing the black one—and we are those with the white ones.

Yet our point in history is called "postmodern," an epoch unlike any other. This is because we are living under the shroud of doubt about *any* happy ending. The sobering threshold into this era has been marked by Holocaust and Hiroshima, followed by a chain reaction of multiple wars for exploitive control. The seasonings for our times are labeled stock market corruption, payoffs in high places, record debt, prohibitive health insurance, environmental crises, grid-locked legislatures, bankruptcies and foreclosures, ongoing Fergusons, and corporate control for greed. Optimistic words once acclaiming easy victory are thrown back in our faces: "Mission Accomplished" and "My answer is, bring them on!" Not surprisingly, many persons have retreated from it all, turning inward in search of happy endings in a private spirituality.

But Scripture refuses to the Christian any such solace, documenting God as continually calling forth disturbing prophets. Yet they in turn, like

Jeremiah, are hunted down as "whistle-blowers," surrounded by plots to "do him in." So dissonant is this vocation of being a prophet that the prophets themselves often rail out against God for "duping" them into thinking that their judgments would birth happy endings. Even the impeccably faithful Jobs are brought to curse the day they were born. And an indelible portrait we have of Jesus is when with bloody Gethsemane sweat he is "filled with fear and great dereliction." And finally he distills our own sense of abandonment with his desolate scream of "Why?".

Although that was back then, Scripture guarantees that still today tailor-made crosses are awarded to each of us with our baptismal certificates. Paul is alarmingly graphic in illustrating with his own life how we will be "regarded as sheep to be slaughtered." Christianity from the beginning has been firmly realistic, insisting that life is not even a B movie, or even a C. The Christian is never given the luxury of living life backwards, having certainty about a confident future that can flow back to guarantee a contented present. The gamble of faith and faith alone is the only honest way of living past promises into a fragile present.

In his book appropriately named *Fear and Trembling*, Kierkegaard's portrayal of the Abraham/Isaac story brings this life of the Christian forcefully home. We so know this event by heart that it becomes diluted into a lovely episode. Equipped with its happy ending, we celebrate Abraham as our model, having passed with an A+ the test of obedience. Yes, but. Abraham undertook his journey with the full intent to murder. God provided him with no other possible ending—just go do it! What we have before us, then, is an horrendous portrait of a cold-blooded father taking his own teenager out into the wilderness to cut his throat with his own bloody hands, and burn the evidence into sacrificial ashes—just because a voice told him to do so! If we would have been present, surely we would have tried to stop him, convinced that he was psychotic, lured not by any God we know but being directed by an evil spirit lurking insanely inside him.

Yet this Abraham-Isaac incident is far from being a singularly bizarre episode. Quite similar is the scriptural portrait of Israel after being liberated from Egypt. We know the happy ending—that they will reach the "promised land." But all the Israelites knew was that Moses had them traipsing all around in endless circles, aimlessly wandering in a hot desert for forty years, just because a stuttering old man said that a voice out of the mouth of a volcano told him to do it! Or consider the similar situation of the disciples. Several of them owned a profitable fishing business, another

II. LIVING THE SEASONS

was a money-spinning tax collector. Yet they just walked away from their boat and their desk to follow an unknown carpenter simply because he said "come," and they came—totally in the dark as to where or why they were going. Seen without their happy endings, it is understandable why the world should regard our faith as absurd, for we are gamblers, with any happy resolution defying the odds.

Okay, but doesn't it matter that we Christians do know how things turn out for such folk as Abraham and the disciples—doesn't that make faith easier for us? No. Theirs was a time in which the earth was flat, a thirty-story tower of Babel threatened to put a hole in the floor of heaven, angels made frequent guest appearances, and anything inexplicable was easily assumed to be a miracle. If anything, faith in our time is even more difficult than in theirs. Utterly beyond their ancient imaginations, we live on a speck of an earth in a cosmos measured by light-years of expanding emptiness, governed by strict laws of cause and effect, where evil spirits have long been abolished by medical science, and pundits expose daily the clay feet of every "saint." With paint remover applied lavishly on all our Christian "likelihoods," we are left more than ever with faith as a naked wager on the basis of hints and rumors.

This is why Lent is so crucial for Christians. It punctures our easy "spirituality" and religious sentimentality by pushing our believing faces into the testing mud of realism. To walk with faithful integrity into Holy Week involves trudging step by step with the only certainty being the inevitability of Maundy Thursday—with an invitation to Jesus' farewell supper before his horrendous execution. Honesty entails for the Christian to return yearly to this experience of forty day and nights without the possibility of resurrection. Sitting at the Jesus table on that final night involves participating at soul depth with Israel's forty years of wandering without sight of a promised land. It involves sitting in silent anguish with Job near his dung heap, bleeding sores from head to toe, stripped clean of every possession, abandoned to mourn the slaughter of his sons and daughters in a deadly tornado. These are the table tears of a haunted night, as we too go out then into the darkness equipped with only a hymn. No wonder we too are tempted to fall asleep rather than witness the Gethsemane pleadings about the cup passing him by—for neither he nor we have certainty about why. And yet with the murderous mob approaching from the valley, and fleeing up over the hill to safety being a ready option, he nevertheless remains and waits. And so do we Christians have any certainty for bearing this Lenten streak of uncertainty, other than living by the wager of faith alone?

And yet, ironically, it is on the far side of our unfeigned Mount of Olives that the gospel breathes its strange life. Not knowing is our knowing, and our hope is in having it stripped away. Based on all empirical evidence, Good Friday provided for the disciples the only possible conclusion—that there was nothing left to do but go fishing. Or trying to get away by taking a Sunday walk to a neighboring town called Emmaus. The meaning of resurrection dawns on those of us undergoing the death of self-sufficiency, when the charge card of our ambitions has been stamped "expired" and "void"— and what we thought was "meaning" is rendered "obsolete." The real Christ appears when the Jolly Green Jesus of our happy endings is swallowed up in the stark common sense of our Holy Saturdays. Our personal pretensions must face death's neutralization; our national arrogance needs nailing to the cross as inanity; and our ecclesiastical superciliousness must undergo its own Golgotha of confession. Only then can we be of good cheer—because in having nothing left about which to cheer we find ourselves at the ironic center of the Christian faith. The very fact that we can persist in wagering on the "impossible dream"—this is likely to be the only evidence that we will ever receive. And yet it is firm because it is not of our own doing. Resurrection is the gift of a faith to live the "nevertheless" in the absence of any certain "becauses." That is when, strangely, we realize that we would rather stand with Jesus and be wrong than to stand anywhere else and be right. Living one's life by gambling on an Easter ending that embraces the whole of creation—what could be more exhilarating?

49. FORTUNATE BETRAYAL

Miracles have never been a ready part of my existence. Perhaps the closest to one occurs when I make soup. When it is time, I empty the refrigerator of everything reaching toward terminality. Wimpy carrots, celery deprived of backbone, potatoes gasping with tentacles—these are the makings. Baptized in spiced broth made from almost forgotten bones, and presto—restoration and redemption called vegetable soup.

Holy Week can feel a bit like that. The pieces seem to show up without much of a recipe—only, in the end, for the whole to redeem the parts. Judas is a leading figure in this speckled drama. Was he a betrayer seduced by money, really? He held the common purse so he could easily have taken off any time for a lush honeymoon with Mary Magdalene. And actually, his payment of thirty pieces of silver wasn't much at all. In fact, after receiving it for doing what he agreed to do, he didn't keep it but threw it in the face of the Council. The reason Scripture gives for his not wanting to keep it is that he came to see that Jesus was innocent. Innocent of what? Really now, what are we to do with Judas? Granted, what he did has the appearance of a terrible thing, and yet it was an indispensable part of the whole redemptive drama. If Judas had not assumed the role of betrayer, then it seems that someone else would have had to do it.

A close reading of the text can give one the feeling that Jesus may have chosen Judas to do it. At the Last Supper, Jesus informed his disciples than an act of betrayal was to be done by the person to whom he gave a morsel of bread. "Am I the one, Rabbi?" Judas asks. Jesus gives him the morsel. Yes. So off he goes, and while the other disciples assumed that he was taking the money purse to go purchase more food, Jesus and Judas understood what had just transpired. Jesus surely knew that when he intentionally overturned the temple money tables just days before the authorities would manage his death. All that remained was for someone to tell them where, "as was his custom," he could be found without any supporting crowds (Luke 22:39 RSV). Then when Jesus was on the Mount of Olives, he saw the mob coming across the valley at a considerable distance. He had at least half an hour in which he could easily have slipped into the darkness, going up the hill to safety with his friends in Bethany on the other side. He chose to be caught.

Yet if we look at what happened this way, what are we to make of Jesus' statement concerning the person who facilitated his crucifixion—that "it would be better if this man had never been born." Yes, it was a terrible burden for Judas to have to bear, to betray his best friend, but surely we are to give thanks to Judas for doing it! The unintended tragedy was that Judas failed—not in what he did but in his being unable to carry his own cross for three days, instead committing suicide when his grief became unbearable, concluding that it was better if he had never been born. Had he persevered by trusting that his part in the drama was somehow essential, then he and Jesus could have embraced knowingly on the other side. A strange interconnect this is Jesus' prearranged suicide in a mutually chosen fratricide. If Judas could have held on for three days without understanding the implications of his doing, he could have experienced the irony that caused Paul to utter in amazement from the perspective of the resurrection: "Shall we sin even more, that grace may abound?" Milton called this irony the "fortunate fall." Judas might then have experienced his own version as the "fortunate betrayal," exclaiming, "Shall I betray him yet again, that the grace of the cross may be even more glorious?" Irony indeed.

Thus while at first glance Holy Week seems composed of strange ingredients without a recipe, we end up celebrating its plot as a gloriously redemptive absurdity. Those of us whose sins are as scarlet are washed whiter than snow, while undeserving prodigals are welcomed home to an Easter breakfast outside an empty tomb. It's craziness, and yet, as it turns out, it seems to have had a plot all along—giving even to our foibles a thankfully inevitable flavor. "Betrayal," then, is a forgivable sin, weavable into the design of God's tapestry. So some day the persons sitting at the right hand of Jesus may not just be Peter, James, and John. Sitting next to Jesus could well be Judas, together smiling, "We did it!"

But we are not there yet. At this point, we are little more than halfway through Holy Week, and the path ahead gets rocky. The Old Testament Breviary reading for this day is from Isaiah. He shares that from birth on, God had been calling him, and us, giving each a special name. And when sometimes he feels that his toil has been in vain, his recompense comes in realizing that all the time it has really been God's doings. "Is it too little," God asks him, "for you to be my servant?" We are the wimpy carrots and spineless celery stalks that somehow are being used by God. Holy Week is our boot camp for learning to trust that, especially when we can't see how or why. So we are to tale it one step at a time, trusting that even of our Gethsemane darkness God is quietly making his soup.

50. LAST SUPPER THAT IS NOT LAST

In my Protestant background, the Thursday of Holy Week was called "Maundy Thursday," meaning "mandate." On that night, we are mandated to remember graphically the Last Supper. A powerful way we did this was ending Holy Communion with a Tenebrae service, meaning "darkness." With thirteen lighted candles on the altar-table, the scriptural story of abandonment and betrayal was read, as one by one the candles representing each disappearing disciple was extinguished. Left alone with only the Christ candle, the final words were spoken, "He breathed his last." A cymbal crash shattered the silence. And the snuffed out last candle plunged us into darkness. "It is finished." Stunned, we were forced to make our uneasy groping toward an exit. All was bleakness—for it was the *Last* Supper.

II. LIVING THE SEASONS

How surprised I was, then, in attending my first Catholic service, for this night was not called "Maundy" but "Holy Thursday." Flowers, bright lights, warm greetings. Instead of a penitential purple, the color was white, complete with Gloria and bells. The tabernacle door was wide open, for nothing was to be held back. What on earth was going on? I learned through a whisper that for Catholics this is not the *Last* Supper but the Lord's Supper—the first of many. Instead of participating in our abandonment of Christ, we were participating in Jesus' promise uttered on that night that "I will not abandon you." From this point in history onward, there would be Christ's ongoing presence with us, because "the bread which I shall give for the life of the world is my flesh." What I came to learn was that Holy Thursday as the first Eucharist is the down payment of Christ's pledge that "he who eats my flesh and drinks my blood abides in me, and I in him." This is the night when Jesus instituted Holy Communion so that we we never again be alone—for "when we break this bread and drink this cup" the incarnation continues, on and on. The elevation of bread and wine is the crucifixion in which our own suffering continues to be nailed with Christ onto the cross, and Easter morning dawning again and again in the "Real Presence" of our corporate communing. "Transubstantiation" is what Catholics call this transaction, understood best not so much in terms of changed elements as in transformed persons. Through the healing power of this ongoing event, sacrifice becomes our liberation, death issues in hope, and God's suffering enables our reconciliation.

Which emphasis is right? Is it too much for us again to hope that they both are? Re-remembering the central event *in* history brings us face-to-face with the last supper of our own death yet to be. Through the central event *of* history, the past becomes an ongoing present of Christ being born now, dying now, and rising now. At the altar of the Last Supper, we are transfixed by the price paid for us then in order for us to celebrate the Lord's Supper of his tabled presence now. Both then and now, a suffering world is being invited into his joyous fellowship—for the one who at the door keeps knocking, promises that if opened, "I will come in to you and eat with you, and you with me" (Rev 3:20 NRSV).

51. FOOT WASHING—DIRTY OR NOT

In some traditions, foot washing is an important part of the Holy Thursday observance, usually with the minister/priest choosing in advance several symbolically representative parishioners to be washed. The Gospel of John portrays Jesus on that night modeling for us how and why we are "to wash one another's feet" (John 13:14 RSV). In fact, when Peter resisted, Jesus was blunt: "If I do not wash you, you have no part in me" (John 13:8 RSV). This drama of servanthood is so powerful that the church has been tempted at times during its history to claim for it the status of sacrament. Yet, ironically, many Christians find the whole idea repugnant. The first time I suggested that my church do it, my lay leader threatened to resign. "No way will I wash someone's stinking feet—yuck." Yet being a Christian is all about doing yuck. Paul was as blunt as Jesus was: "When reviled, we bless; when persecuted we endure; when slandered, we try to conciliate; we have become and are now, as the refuse of the world, the offscourings of all things" (1 Cor 4:13 RSV).

A powerful portrait of yuck is Michelangelo's Pieta in which Mary holds on her lap the mutilated corpse of her son, staining her hands and garment with blood. Numerous are paintings portraying St. Francis's breakthrough to the heart of the gospel when he found himself finally able to kiss the feet of a leper. Classic in our time is the photograph of Mother Theresa embracing with a kiss a dying AIDS victim. "Truly I tell you, just as you did it to one of the least of these who are members of my family, you did it to me" (Matt 25:40 NRSV). In this world that Christ claims as family, those whom Jesus finds to be yucky are those who regarding themselves as being the "most," thereby above serving the "least." Somehow, to be a Christian has to do with yuck.

Some years ago I was appointed to the United Methodist Conference Board of Ordained Ministry, only to find that it had become nastily split theologically. The hostility began splashing over into our interviews with prospective candidates for ordination. Feeling that the situation was becoming reckless, we who were in leadership dared to plan an overnight retreat that would force either reconciliation or an irreconcilable fracture. It began with a supper in which we knew our problem would become visible—when the members predictably self-selected themselves into "liberal" and "conservative" tables. That evening we gathered in a room made into a chapel, taking turns reading and then reflecting on select Scriptures about forgiving rather than judging, on loving one's enemies as one's self (e.g., Luke 6:32–38 RSV). This sharing softened us a bit in preparation for a communal-style Holy Communion, concluding with Jesus' prayer for his church: "That they may be one, as we are one" (John 17:22 NRSV).

II. LIVING THE SEASONS

With fear and trembling, we read off the list of roommates, carefully selected into duos least likely to be compatible. With a nervous benediction, we sent them off.

We survived the night, and at breakfast the seating was noticeably more "integrated," with conversations seasoned by laughter. After paired-off walks, by midmorning the interaction seemed sufficiently positive for us to muster courage to follow through with our planned final event—the washing of feet. We read aloud the account of Jesus washing the feet of his disciples on the final night of his life, ending with his command: "You also ought to wash one another's feet" (John 13:14 NRSV). Not daring to make this compulsory, the executive committee began—gingerly, for this was a first for us too. Each of us chose a theological opposite as a partner, and asked permission to wash their feet. No one refused, although the agreement was a low-grade whisper. Then, very gently, in our darkened room lit by candlelight, we invited any who might be willing to do the same. Slowly the miracle began unfolding. Not only were there no abstainers, but instead of choosing friends, each chose a former opponent. When all had participated, the hugging was spontaneous—and vigorous. Then one of the most "difficult" members of the board was moved to pick up his Bible and complete the story: "A new commandment I give to you, that you love one another; even as I have loved you . . ." (John 13:34 RSV). If we define a sacrament as a redemptive act instituted by Jesus, we may need to reconsider the status of Jesus' Maundy Thursday modeling—the mutual washing of yucky feet to the glory of God.

52. GOOD FRIDAY AND THE DEFINING THREE MOMENTS

The "big bang," we are told, occurred in a split second. For the Christian, the destiny of humankind was virtually determined by three seconds. This was how long it took for that infamous Friday to become "Good." Our scene is the crucifixion of the one named Jesus. The first of these three moments begins with a shriek of pain-tortured dereliction. Ricocheting against the silent heavens, it is the definitive "why question" that has plagued humanity from the first moment of human consciousness. The cosmic bang and the cosmic scream are hyphenated. "My God, my God, *why* have you forsaken me?" (Mark 15:34 NRSV). Forsaken *us*! This cry resounds out into ever expanding space, as if the earth is holding its breath on tiptoe, as "darkness came over the whole land" (Mark 15:33 NRSV). Then comes the second instant—a terrifying silence, in which "the earth shook" (Matt 27:51 RSV). Isaiah describes tersely its character: "All flesh is grass . . . . The grass withers, the flower fades" (Isa 40:6-7 RSV). All things finite end in pathos.

This second moment is the only honest conclusion to be drawn empirically about our human destiny. Death marinated in various shades of suffering awaits us all. Only the individual timetables differ. My God why? Why live, why life, why bother, why anything—for they give slow death stride of the womb as grave? Is this void the ultimate finality—or penultimate? Is this all there is?

Wait, it depends on whether there is a third instant. His lips move, imperceptible at first, and then he shouts "with a loud voice, 'Father, into your hands I commit my spirit!'" (Luke 23:46). Incredible. These final words of Jesus defy human logic—as a "nevertheless." In spite of all evidence to the contrary, at the threshold of a torturous death, Jesus is able to trust. As he had striven to do throughout his life, now at the end he remains trusting that behind the blood-stained curtain is a God who is trustworthy. Rejected, betrayed, and deserted, yet he died trusting God: "Father, into you hands . . ." (Luke 23:46 NRSV). The universe breathes as in a gasp of relief. Only then, in a profound sense, "It is finished" (John 19:30 RSV).

If it were not for Jesus, I would be an atheist. I cannot do what he did; I cannot believe what he believed; I cannot trust what he trusted. The second moment would have saturated my world—for the third possibility stands on the other side of the chasm that I cannot bridge. On one side is the "because." On the other is the "nevertheless." On my own, there is no way that I can get from one side to the other. I cannot. In me there is no bridge from nothingness to hope, from suffering to trust, from death to life. That is why I am a Christian. *Faith means trusting the Jesus who was able to trust God as Father.* For better or for worse, Jesus and I are in it together, all the way.

A powerful prayer from the breviary confesses this strikingly: "Lord, Jesus, you were rejected by your people, betrayed by the kiss of a friend, and deserted by your disciples. Give us the confidence that you had in the Father, and our salvation will be assured" [*The Liturgy of the Hours*, NY, Catholic Book Publishing Co., vol. IV, p. 871].

Right or wrong, the Christian stands with Jesus. If it turns out that he was deluded, that the cosmos is empty after all, then his cry shall be our mutual protest against the meaninglessness of our cosmic abandonment. Whichever, we are in it together, for there is no one else in all of creation with whom I would rather stand to encounter the "Why" than with the trusting Jesus.

53. GOOD FRIDAY AND THE WAY OF THE CROSS

I arrive in Jerusalem on a Friday afternoon. I have three days to see the city, without a clue as to where to go. I spy a sign with an arrow pointing towards a "Catholic Information Center." I manage only one question before the kindly lady behind the counter pushes me toward the door. "Take that alley, go down the stairs, and turn at the first left. You'll see a group just starting the Stations of the Cross." It is Friday at three o'clock. I run. I find. I join.

Tradition has named "stations" in Jerusalem where something of consequence happened to Jesus on his Good Friday—the "Way of the Cross" it is called. The first station marks the spot where he is condemned to die by Pilate. Each Ash Wednesday the burned palms from last year's celebration of Jesus' triumphant entry are smeared on our foreheads as a dirty cross of confession. Had we been watching along this path 2,000 years ago, odds are that we too would have been shouting for this "terrorist's" crucifixion.

So here I am, centuries later, being drawn into walking the walk as a Franciscan brother talks the talk, himself dragging a heavy cross. I follow through the narrow streets as irritated merchants push us away from blocking entry to their wares. Unreal, like a home video, but the props are real. As we stop at each station for prayer, the shorthand names began identifying something of my own pilgrimage. "Condemned," "carry," "falls," "mother," "help," "compassion," "falls again," "women," "falls yet again," "gamble," "crucified," "died," "descent," and "buried." Fourteen in all. Halfway through these stations, our pilgrimage leads into an old church. Turning sharply right, we climb some steep stairs. One by one the persons in front of me put a hand into a hole in the stone floor. "What's happening," I whisper. "Shhhhh—it's where the cross stood." I feel goose bumps. I am not prepared for this.

Then, in single file, we descend by another staircase, and slowly move toward a strange cave-like formation located on the main floor of the church. Silently, folks wait in line—I had no idea what for. Each person is going alone through a low narrow opening, and half a minute later each reemerges. Nervously, it is my turn. I stoop and go in. There is a low antechamber. Forced to bow a second time, I enter a smaller space with a stone ledge. On it sits a Franciscan monk. "Where am I?" I ask. His whisper seems thunderous. "The tomb of Jesus." I hardly remember anything more. Eventually I stumble back out into the dimness, tempted to warn those waiting to enter. I sit on the church floor in a dark corner, for a long time. I do not know what to make out of this, nor what to do with my feelings. I am "there."

Friends had told me that my visit to Jerusalem would be disappointing—because tradition claims to know too much. "The streets are probably not paved with the actual stone." "The route probably isn't exactly correct . . ." "The places are arbitrary." But here I am, and it doesn't matter. Close enough. Maybe too close. I had only known "about" these things. Now I am strangely part of them. I had entered as Mary Magdalene had entered, when she "saw a young man sitting on the right side, dressed in a white robe." My man had a brown robe, but it doesn't matter. In effect, he told me the same thing that she had been told: "He is not here; see the place where they laid him" (Mark 16:6).

In one hour I had walked through Good Friday. And here I sit, in a cold, damp, dark corner of an ancient church, blown away by a Good Friday now my own. Everything depends on believing the rest of the message: "He has risen, he is not here." At the moment I am experiencing the "not here part"—the feel of life without Easter.

54. GOOD FRIDAY—FUNERALS AND BEYOND

Perhaps the favorite phrase in the church's vocabulary is "good news," a translation of the word "gospel." But what makes good "good"? Let's begin with the easy part, the "bad news." Distilled in a sentence, life is tragic because it is circumscribed by sickness unto death. Our society conspires to hide the ultimate empirical truth—that each of us will die. Soft music at a lovely "funeral parlor," linen sheets on a mattressed coffin of crafted walnut, a final vault protecting the person from the earth and its rains. The best-kept secret is the one-way door behind the drapes at the end of the corridor, marked "point of no return." The Good Friday liturgy tears open that secret, dogged in its insistence that truly good news is available only on the far side of the bad. Scripture provides us no hiding, for at least half of each Gospel deals with Jesus' tragic three-day death walk.

At the monastery, the priest's chasuble for Good Friday is blood red, marked with a black cross. The night before, the church overflowed with flowers in joyful celebration of the Lord's Supper, the last time as the first time. Now all of that is swept away, the church stripped, nothing left, everything gone—the place ravished. The tabernacle door gapes wide open, as if the jewels in the family safe have been stolen. In preparation for this mid-afternoon happening, our lunch is bread and water, treating us as if we are prisoners condemned to our own execution. We enter the chilled church with bare feet, quickly engulfed in the tragedy. Standing for what seems an interminable time, the whole of the long Holy Week narrative is read. "Crucify him!" we shout. Finally the primal words are spoken: "He breathed his last." Falling to the floor, we assume a cruciform posture of our own—silent, very still, our faces pushed into the hardness of the cold floor. So this is what crucifixion is like.

After an unbearable time, we arise—only to have the liturgy force us to do the most ridiculous thing imaginable. Gazing at the crucified Jesus hanging of a cross like a plucked chicken, we are to intercede in his name for every type of human being in the world, nailing our prayers onto his cross in desperate hope. How bizarre—inviting the dead one through us to embrace the world. Our intercessions go on and on, for at least ten minutes, praying first for the church; then for church leaders; and clergy; and laity; for those preparing for baptism; for the unity of all Christians; for Jews; for all who do not believe in Christ; for those who do not believe in God; for those with special needs; and finally we pray even for politicians—"through Christ our Lord." The whole world is wrapped with us in this human tragedy, each of us, all of us—for his fate is ours.

What follows punctuates even further our plight, as a rugged cross is unwrapped in our presence and held high—the death of God. Equipped with only a promise that stands in bold relief to death's strapping evidence, our Good Friday observance climaxes with a wild invitation to wager on the "impossible." One by one we come forward, kneel, and kiss the nail plunged through his feet. This kiss of faith is our fragile effort to cancel the kiss of betrayal that we share with Judas. "My people, my people, what have I done to you," cries out the abandoned God. The hymn is stark: "Precious Lord, take my hand . . . tired . . . worn . . . storm . . . night . . . cry . . . fell . . . darkness . . . home." Then it is all over—for the time being.

Holy Saturday is the day of devastation—when we are to live out the Good Friday implications. The day of dreams, crushed by death's final harshness. Nothing is left, for the disciples and for us, except to live as fact Paul's definitive logic: "If Christ has not been raised, our preaching is in vain and your faith is in vain of content and your faith is empty" (1 Cor

15:14 RSV). Gaining such clarity about our human condition is why we need this yearly return to Golgotha.

And Easter? The elaborate music and lily bit can be disconcerting, even misleading. Instead, the heart of Easter emerges best for me, perhaps, at funerals. The coffin is sprinkled with water and draped symbolically with the white gown worn at one's baptism—acting out the full implications of immersion. Having been submerged three times into the water of Christ's three-day tomb, one's death has become lived for us, by the one who precedes us in all things—this time in resurrection. So wrapped in promise, the coffin is brought to the altar as a gift returned to God with thanks—as with gusto the congregation sings, "Jesus Christ is Risen Today." The Christian funeral is our Easter way of informing death that it did not win. The last word belongs to another.

55. A HELLISH GOD

Because certain parts of Jesus' life are so hard to understand, our interpretations can vary radically. More than anything, our versions reflect what we need for them to mean. The most unfathomable of all, perhaps, is Christ's cry of dereliction from the cross. Perhaps saints can get maudlin about it because some of them may never have known serious doubt, or experienced stern separation from God. Even martyrs may not have grasped the fullness of what is involved, for many of them apparently experienced joy in being "chosen" for crucifixion with Christ. Those more likely to understand are those who through guilt have tasted the God-forsakenness of the psalmist: "Against thee, thee only, have I sinned, and done that which is evil in thy sight" (Ps 51:4 RSV). Or those who like Cain who can only whisper, "My punishment is greater than I can bear" (Gen 4:13 RSV). The Peters likewise have a strong clue—those who after three denials have had Jesus turn to look them straight in the heart, and "went out and wept bitterly" (Luke 22:62 RSV) Then there are the Judases who realize that they "have sinned in betraying innocent blood," and in presumed forsakenness see suicide as the only way out (Matt 27:4 RSV).

These are among the folks most likely to be grasped by the incredible implications of Christ's derelict cry. Jesus was suffering absolute severance from God because he was taking on the sins of the whole world as his very own—in utter aloneness. So, on second thought, no one is able to grasp fully what is at stake. The cosmic scream of Jesus is beyond anything we can imagine, for this singular cry erupts from the strangled depth of all humanity. And yet at this very same moment, it is a cry issuing from the very center of God's own soul. None of us can understand. We can only stand in silent awe—that very God of very God is experiencing within his own being, for us, that heart of abandonment called hell. And to be grasped by even a hint of what is going on is to hear if only faintly the sound of a mantra that through the ages retains its constant beat: for "lo, I am with you always, to the close of the age" (Matt 28:20 RSV).

56. HELL AND HOLY SATURDAY

Holy Saturday is a strange day. The church provides us no liturgy for it, perhaps being too bewildered to conceive one. As a result, we can easily squander its meaning, busily preparing the Easter ham for tomorrow's feast. So Holy Saturday may be no big deal, for we know that everything will turn out okay, and soon. But for the disciples, this Saturday beyond all others is anything but holy. With punctured dream, the disciples have nothing left but to go back to fishing, and even monks just go back to work.

But there is an intriguing ancient tradition that provides rare power to the meaning of this day. We are taken to a scene behind the scene, a drama beneath the drama. This event became officially recognized in the ninth century when the church added to the Apostles' Creed these words: "He descended into hell." The abode of the dead. The meaning of this affirmation is to proclaim with full force the incredible breadth of the good news—that Christ's redemption is retroactive, wrapping back to embrace those who died before his coming. Holy Saturday is the day when Jesus himself enters the abode of death and embraces the dead, providing for every human being an equal opportunity for forgiveness and eternal life.

During the Middle Ages, this event expanded in power, coming to be called the "harrowing of hell." Christ tore from its hinges the locked gates of Hades itself. An ancient homily for Holy Saturday goes all the way by portraying the crucified Christ as going in search of Adam and Eve, and all the lost sheep through the ages. And finding them, the embrace is of long-lost friends. With spittle still on his face and nail wounds covering his body, Christ whispers fondly to the primal couple and their offspring: "I did not create you to be held a prisoner in hell . . . rise, let us leave this place, for you are in me and I am in you." He knows the way—and has the key.

I would like to believe that he also calls by name the one standing sullenly in the shadow. "Judas!" Arm in arm they leave, with Jesus murmuring, "I could not have done it without you!" Jesus knows the route—out past the rolled-away stone, onto a path leading to a homecoming banquet for prodigals and lost sheep. This is the Easter feast at which the fatted calf is celebrated as being none other than the lamb slain from the foundation of the world—for Judas, and thus for us too. It is this vision that the Eucharistic feast salutes in foretaste.

57. HOLY SATURDAY AND THE "SURE THING"

I keep being drawn back to Holy Saturday. Yes, it is the day when the bottom falls out. And yet, if we again block out our knowing how things will turn out, Holy Saturday takes on the realistic flavor of "no-but-maybe-though-unlikely-yet-perchance." Then it is that we can realize how many of us Christians are really Holy Saturday folk. We live much of our days dangling out there somewhere between nothingness and everything, as we gamble our few red chips on improbables and unlikelies. Even our Easter mornings have something of this honest flavor, as when Peter and John race to the empty tomb, and find nothing—or was it everything? Like them, should we sanely return quietly to our homes, perplexed without understanding? Or should we make a fool of ourselves dancing at the mouth of an empty tomb? Faith always lives in ambivalence, depriving us for life of any "sure thing," always uncertain about those things that are of most importance.

Yet there is something intoxicating about such Holy Saturday living, teased by this elusiveness of a "yes but maybe not," of "why but why not?" It is this Christian tension that keeps the shroud of life's negativity from stifling us. Though nothing is certain, the titillation of Easter hope can give to every disappointment an edge of "nonetheless," a quivering of "maybe not yet." This may be why Christians keep rooting for the underdog. I have no personal animosity against the New England Patriots, but how fine when they get upset! A friend with good humor wisely asked me last week, "Can a Christian really be a Yankees fan?"

Christianity is about the biggest of upsets, the three-pointer at the buzzer, the Hail Mary at the whistle—with Paul serving as our franchise announcer, screaming "Unbelievable!" To our end, hope and doubt will always sit side by side, causing us at times to wonder if the game is over, is happening, or is yet to be played. Holy Saturday existence has the titillating feel of living hopefully on the edge of the improbable—cheering for forgiveness over retaliation, gentleness over violence, peace over war, love over hate, hope over despair, self-giving over self-seeking, life over death, God over nothingness.

Without "the next day," Abraham would have been guilty of manslaughter. Without the next day, Jesus would have been a heartbroken dreamer. Without the next day, the disciples would have been naive fools. Without Easter, we Christians have been duped. For the Christian, there is always a "next day." Faith tantalizes the world's Saturday living with edgings of inklings. Whether to live the boring innocuousness of a sure thing, or gamble the exhilaration of rooting for the underdog to pull off an upset—isn't that a no-brainer?

58. MARSHMALLOW EASTER

The greeting some pastors address to their crowded Easter congregations has become a cliché: "Merry Christmas! I won't be seeing many of you until then, so let me be the first to say it." It is surprising how indifferent many of us Christians can be about our faith, even as a growing band of pundit atheists resembling Roman soldiers are today approaching Jesus with verbal spit, taunt, and insult. It seems that the majority of us take Pilate's approach—cloaking with a "magnificent robe" his tortured body, and then surrendering him to the crowds to do as they will. The churches must take some responsibility for this when they offer happily orchestrated bell choir Easter services, infested with lilies sufficient to match the congregation's finery. It is hard to imagine any production more cosmetically adept at hiding what a handful of the congregation went through on Good Friday and the day after.

Even as a boy I was puzzled when I found in my Easter basket a chocolate-covered cross filled with marshmallow. While the Easter bunny may be theologically sluggish, the Easter portrait we find in John's gospel for the day is anything but marshmallowy. We have a tear-strickened Mary Magdalene, utterly alone, outside the tomb of her beloved. She hears a voice, and as she turns toward it, we might well expect a Hollywood finale. Surely with her strong profile caught in streaming sunlight, the music will crescendo as she and Jesus race into each other's arms, ecstatically embracing as friends never again to be parted! But no, it isn't like that at all. She does not even recognize him! He is bruised and scarred beyond all recognition. No chocolate coating here.

Part of our Easter shallowness may relate to our inability, or unwillingness, to imagine the terror of crucifixion. The closest I have come to it was in witnessing the execution of a prisoner I believed to be innocent—but even this was nowhere close. The scene is utterly sanitized by the prison as preparations are done behind closed blinds. His mother and I waited, just waited—carefully watched by guards. Suddenly the Venetian blinds blink open, and in a blaze of light we see an utterly white room designed to impress us with cleanliness. There is my friend on a gurney, his black face tucked in with a sheet as if in preparation for a blissful sleep. Our eyes meet. I wink. I wave. I mouth my love. The blinds close with a thud. Fifteen seconds. It's over! I had seen murder happen—denial style.

No such blinds cloak the crucifixion of Jesus. There are no drugs administered for pain, no soundproof room to stifle the screams, no sterile white environment to tidy up a killing choreographed for public consumption. No, with Jesus there is only blatant torture. Instead of injection needles, there are railroad spikes. Didn't they at least provide a footrest on the cross? Yes—in order to stretch out the horrendous pain for as long as possible. We are told that the harshest part of crucifixion is the burning thirst. "I thirst." Researchers all conclude that what Jesus endures is the cruelest kind of dying that humankind has ever designed—orchestrated by Rome to be so excruciating that no one would dare be a disciple of this spectacle on the hill called "the Skull."

Even more, what Jesus sees as he looks out with dazed eyes from the cross is an appalling cross section of society—a typical television audience. The spectrum ranges from the jealously mean-spirited taunts of religious leaders, to six-pack spectators seeking amused diversion, to opportunists hustling bets on how long he will survive. The mob's cheers encourage abuse. This is great entertainment drawing eager crowds, as hucksters turn such events into carnivals for profit and fun—drawing many who had gained their jollies less than a week ago with a Palm Sunday parade. His crucified companion on the one side shouts insults at him; the one on the other side seeks a final favor.

Here we see the one who had fed the repressed hopes of vast crowds, now feeding to life their baser instincts. Executions are devised to last three or four days. Jesus fails them even here. By dying within hours, the entertainment he provides is little longer than a Sunday afternoon football game with double overtime. The throng had come prepared to stay for the long haul, several days of being beguiled and mesmerized by the hemorrhaging, the convulsions of head, lungs, and limbs—and finally hours of slow screaming death from excruciating thirst and hunger. Then, after gangrene claims the body, it is left as a spectacle on the cross, rotting as birds pick out the eyes and eat at the remains, leaving only a hideous skeleton as warning. None of our horror movies can rival this.

But Jesus deprives them of their show. What a letdown. Jesus has failed even as a failure! Without warning, with hardly time to focus a camera, he utters a terrifying scream, and dies—of a broken heart. What a cheat, worth demanding one's money back. And even the spectacle of his dripping remains are quickly taken away from them. He has failed religiously as well, an embarrassment to be hidden from the Passover celebration.

Oh yes, then what about Easter? Easter is nailed inseparably to Good Friday. In a strange sense, Easter occurs as a question—at the point of Christ's cry in the Good Friday liturgy. As we are stretched out on the floor in the front of a cross, becoming a cruciformed acting out of humanity's common fate with the crucified one, the question of questions forcefully arises. Who is He, really? Really! Some say Elijah. Some say John the Baptist. Some say, "Hey, who?" "But who do you say that I am?" That is *the* question. Easter is our wagered response, with or without lilies.

59. THE EYES HAVE IT

Paul vowed to preach nothing except Jesus Christ and him crucified. He understood that Easter is so hyphenated with Good Friday that the Easter good news has to do with crosses. For much of my life I misunderstood crosses—and thus crucifixion. In my mind's eye, I saw the crucifixion as ethereal, spiritual, much as in an El Greco painting, with Jesus high and lifted up above the earth. At other times, the image in my mind resembles Rubens's version, our perspective being that of looking down powerfully with Jesus from above the human scene. "Lift High the Cross," sings the joyful hymn. Jesus himself indicated as much, that "when I am lifted up from the earth I will draw all people to myself" (John 12:32 NRSV). Yet such imagery can be misleading.

Crosses are deliberately constructed to be low, with the feet of the crucified only a foot from the ground. This is to encourage spectators to become participants. Taunting by the soldiers provides only a tame prelude as invitation, giving permission for throwing stones at the crucified as a target. Then a daring person will venture to run up and kick at the body, turning with a laugh and raised fist to receive cheers. Crucifixions are designed to bring out the worst in people. Since the helpless victim cannot fight back, it is a totally safe way of spewing all kinds of pent-up anger, drawing roars of approval from the spectator crowd. Nothing is forbidden. Our American version is lynching.

When I let my imagination wrap itself around this portrait, the image of eyes obsesses me. Persons could walk straight up to Jesus, thrusting sticks into his mouth and ears. But my mind fixates on those who dared to thrust their face into his, no more than an inch away. Then looking him straight in the eye, they spit. Eyes looking into eyes can say so much—from hatred to reconciliation, from intimidation to love, from seduction to compassion.

I am particularly humbled by eyes during Holy Communion. As persons come forward to receive, I look each in the eye, extending the body of the crucified one at eye level. Some communicants resemble the tax collector, their eyes bowed toward the floor: "Have mercy on me a sinner." Others resemble Peter after the cock crowed, just staring as if glazed. A few give hints of the self-righteous Pharisee, trying to stare Jesus down. Many cannot, or will not, look me in the eye at all. But with those who do, we smile. "The body of Christ." It is an instant of resurrection. The smile of the Christian conveys even to the stranger that they are not alone.

This may be why I prefer John's version of Easter. Mary Magdalene has the courage to remain in the tomb garden after the other disciples have left. They had seen nothing but nothing. But she hears a voice, but not really, for she regards it as only the gardener. No sight recognition, no voice recognition. But hearing her name, she turns and their eyes meet. Then she knows. "Rabboni!" A friend of mine daily visits his wife who has Alzheimer's, looking long and intently into her eyes, as she stares back. One day I asked incredulously: "Does she really know who you are?" "Not likely, but I know who she is."

One's whole life is a preparation to look into the eyes of Jesus, sometime, somewhere, whatever the disguise. Will we dare to look him in the eye? Or will we have to cringe, looking down at the floor? Will we take a sideways glance to check out our odds? Will we flinch at his glance, angry at his apparent abandonment? Will we stare at the ceiling in avoidance? What will it be like? Easter will have dawned for us if we find ourselves gifted with courage sufficient to look into his bloodshot eyes without turning away. If

Scripture is to be trusted, his response will be a smile—a smile the size of the universe. "Welcome home." But such looking will take practice—gained daily by looking into the eyes of others the way we hope he is already looking into ours.

60. DUM DE DUM DUM

During our noontime eating at the monastery, one of the monks reads to the rest of us from a book chosen by the abbot. This is another way of acting out our incarnational intersecting of body and spirit. Besides choosing the text, an abbatial prerogative is ringing the closing bell whenever he chooses—even if that entails half a banana in one's mouth, or cutting off the reader in mid-sentence. One Holy Week the bell sounded just as the reader read this sentence: "Will the Emperor be able to withstand the attack from without or not?" Ding-dong—and there we were, dangling in suspense. I whispered to my table mate, "Well, will he or won't he?" He responded, "Dum de dum dum, tune in tomorrow and see if Superman can save Lois from a fate worse than death!" Ah, those childhood moments when a radio serial ended abruptly, leaving us on the suspenseful edge of the impossible.

Our lively faith is a bit like that. The Bible is composed of a series of suspenseful events, each ending with the haunting question, "Now what? Stay tuned!" After my monk friend's response recalled my childhood memory, Holy Week became interestingly perky that year. On Tuesday, the Gospel ends with Peter's insistence to Jesus, "I will lay down my life for you!" Jesus replies, "O really, before the cock crows you will betray me three times!" "Will he or won't he? Dum de dum dum. Stay tuned." Wednesday the spotlight shifts to Judas, ending with the words "Surely it is not I, Rabbi." "Will he betray Jesus, or not? Dum de dum dum. Stay tuned." On Thursday Jesus elaborates the model life that his disciples are to follow. "But will they, or won't they? Dum de dum dum. Stay tuned." They didn't, ushering us tragically into Friday. "They laid him in a tomb that was close by." "Is that all there is? Dum de dum dum. Stay tuned."

Wearily we reach Easter Vigil, the three-hour biggie that will surely provide the definitive resolution. But alas what we hear is of disciples who, hearing a strange story from women about an empty tomb, "refused to believe." Desperate, Peter breathlessly runs to see for himself. "But could see nothing . . . ? Is such emptiness the climax? Dum de dum dum. Stay tuned." Certainly in the morning we will know, won't we, one way or another? The music mounts, the suspense rises, an Easter crescendo is surely at hand. We rise expectantly to hear the Easter day Scripture, this time from a different Gospel. But all we are given is the story of John in a competitive footrace with Peter, bewildered when in entering a barren tomb they slink away to an enigmatic editorial: "They did not yet understand the Scripture, that he had to rise from the death." "Dum de dum dum—will they come to understand, or not? Stay tuned."

Staying tuned, that's what it's all about. Episode after episode, day after day, year after year, for the long haul. "Will we be faithful, or not? Dum de dum dum. Stay tuned." Lincoln at Gettysburg wisely declared that whether or not those who died there would have done so in vain depended on the actions of his listeners. The "gods" who once roamed Greece and protected the Roman Empire are now quaint oddities. So might it be with Christianity, for we are the ones who are determining whether the crucified one has died in vain. Deprived of all certainty, the Christian walks by faith as a participant in a narrative that is ongoing—an adventure of apprehension and never comprehension, pursued in hopeful suspense, with the determining ending yet to be. Stay tuned.

61. EASTER STORIES

Easter occurs in dissimilar ways for diverse folks. It happened for two of the disciples simply by taking a long walk, meeting a stranger who questioned them about the adequacy of the plot they assumed their life was taking. The story they had told the stranger was a tragedy. But the re-story that he told had the power to awaken in them the makings of a comedy (Luke 24:13ff). For many of us, however, the dilemma goes even deeper. Our lives are so segmented that they seem destitute of *any* plot. Therefore becoming a Christian begins by discovering that each of our lives indeed has a plot, known or unknown—and whatever the details, its anatomy is most likely that of a tragedy. "Conversion" occurs, as with the two hiking disciples, in being aroused to discern how one's story line is transformed by being taken up into the divine plot.

The heart of the gospel is not primarily about the characteristics of Jesus or about his teachings. What matters is the defining plot of the "Christ event" in which Jesus is the primal actor, disclosing the cosmic liturgy in which God is the defining Celebrant. Each human life has a thread holding together one's days and nights, quietly being woven into the emerging pattern of the divine tapestry. Discerning this design is a christological adventure in which the character of the Weaver is disclosed. Faith means wagering that the thread of one's life is a vital subplot being embroidered into the meaning of the whole.

We Christians don't hear much anymore about "testifying," as was the expectation at Wednesday evening "Prayer Meetings." Yet testimonies address two questions that remain as germane today as ever. First, when did life cave in for you—whether hefty or undersized? Translated this means when and how did things such as guilt, depression, abandonment, failure, or disappointment become your Good Friday? Second, when and how did Easter hope dawn for you? That is, when did someone function as Christ for you, appearing when you most needed help—so that you could hear birds singing in the graveyard? One's two answers serve as the perigee and apogee of the scenario profiling one's lived meaning.

Often the shallowness of plot that many persons are living reflects a failure to face head-on the tragic nature of unredeemed life. But even more, the crisis of our age resides not only with the number of persons who have lost meaning in their living, but in how many of them are oblivious or even indifferent to the loss. Consequently the vehicles for awakening often need to be harsh. The eye-opening began for one of my friends when the diagnosis was a brain tumor. For another, it was a severe heart attack. In both cases, their awakening came as a fracturing of their obsessive drivenness for acknowledgement, accomplishment, and ambition. For another friend, getting serious about this matter of living transpired when an ankle fractured during a fast break with neighborhood kids brought his illusory dream with the Lakers to a sobering standstill. For still another, an accomplished freelance photographer was rendered vocationally obsolete by technology. For another, the awakening began when anger at her dead mother began slopping over to poison her other relationships—until in one throbbing episode she saw her mother in herself. This menagerie of deflations are all variations on what occurred to the disciples—in which resurrection occurred only on the other side of puncturing.

Yet when our awaking begins, even when the reversal happens, our Good Fridays remain. Authentic Easters are not coping mechanisms. They are not spiritual vitamins for supplying with more energy the life we have been living. Easter means nothing less than a renovation of a life experienced as distasteful, unsustainable, or hollow. Easter is not a prize, a reward for a life of calculated planning and determined discipline. It is incapable of being deserved or even expected. The road from Good Friday to Easter is permanently cut off at the pass by an avalanche of our own doings. Where we find ourselves being, then, is distilled well in the liturgy. As the body of Christ is being held up before our eyes, one confession is a one-liner: "Lord, I am not worthy to receive you, but only say the word and I shall be healed." "Grace" means being humbled by God's incredible graciousness—of forgiveness, of acceptance, of love. This gift of healing is what it means to participate in the resurrection that is Easter.

When Israel reached its Good Friday impasse in being exiled as slaves from their own land, the psalmist cried out their only hope: "If I forget you, O Jerusalem, let my right hand wither!" (Ps 137:5 RSV). So is the cry of the Christian: "If in my Good Friday exiles I forget my soul-aching cravings for Easter, let depression wither my life! And if in my Easter joys I forget my Good Friday humblings, let my Easters wither into rootless sentimentality!" There is no real Easter without a Lenten flavor, and no Lent without an Easter yearning. Even without ashes on their foreheads, one can identify Christians by the way they look at the horizon.

62. THE TOMB AS CAVE

Plato portrays our human dilemma as that of sitting in a cave, our backs to the light streaming in from the entrance. Thus we see the real happenings outside the cave only as reflected shadows on the back wall, mistaking silhouettes for reality. Conversion entails turning around, amazed in peering out through the entrance into the real world in all its beauty. For the Christian, that cave is our empty tomb. Unless our turning establishes a radical change in perspective, we will keep looking at the wall, rehearsing the recurring shadows of failures, disappointments, and hurts—as they filter the light coming through the entrance at our backs. Thus the newness of each "now" is squandered—for in being strained through our past, we remain a shadow of who we were meant to be.

When Peter and John entered the cave-tomb, they saw in the shadowed light only a linen shroud and a folded napkin. Just as Mary Magdalene, they too backed out, as it were, having looked in the wrong direction. What they saw was so filtered that all they could think was "who stole the body . . . , tell me . . . and I will take him away" (John 20:14–15 RSV). Mary had entered the cave with eyes intent on anointing the dead. Only when she

II. LIVING THE SEASONS

turned toward the cave entrance, did she see him in the real world with all its gardened beauty.

For a sizable portion of my life, my filtered perspective tended to see this central portion of the Christian narrative only through skeptical questions: "How can a dead man walk out of his grave?" The obvious answer was that he could not. As this working assumption was intensified during college, my childhood faith was perforated. My tomb-cave turnaround began only when one day I found myself asking questions of another sort. "One way or another, would resurrection make any difference?" The transforming conclusion was that indeed it would. Resurrection is the name for a dream embedded deeply inside each of us—the ache that "even though I walk through the valley of the shadow of death . . . thou art with me" (Ps 23:4 RSV). This yearning is for a God who shares our crying and pain, faces down our death, and promises that "those who sow in tears [will] reap with shouts of joy!" (Ps 126:5). But in having only the empirical back wall at which to stare, the carnival of shadows cumulatively raises the nightmare question: "Is this all there is?"

No, there is more, much more. And those who are turned toward the tomb's opening can taste a dawn choreographed by the God whose resurrection promise is "to make all things new." Making the turn is the cusp on which the vision of resurrection teeters.

Recently, in rereading some of the articles I have written over the years, I was amazed at how often I used the phrase, "What if . . . ?" I shouldn't have been surprised. Every human being, inevitably, is a person of "faith," with the difference depending on which "what if" we wager on. We all live subjunctively—living "as if" something is true about which we can never know for sure, gambling that it will provide our lives with a meaning worth living. Nothing in life is certain, except death—and in the face of death we are risking our lives on something that can never be a sure thing.

None of the many Christians I have known have had the certainty of a "supernatural" experience that separated them off from non-believers. From atheist to believer, we all live by hints followed by guesses, by the rumble of rumors—experiences not ostensibly different in kind from those that unbelievers have had. In all honesty, what Christians gamble upon as graciously divine intrusions may simply be the first whippoorwill in spring, romping in autumn leaves, smelling the fresh soup, being mesmerized by fog massaging a responsive valley, or watching a giggling child being loved by the tongue of a new puppy. These are the Easter hints blowing in from the entrance, coaxing us to make a turn about-face from the soiled picture screen on our cave-tomb's back wall. We all live in an empty tomb. What matters is the direction that we face.

63. EASTER SAVORING

One thing that puzzles me about my brother monks is how hurried some of them are in finishing their meal. They seem to gobble it down, as if too impatient to savor the experience. I find this behavior especially strange on Sundays when our noon meal is trimmed with ice cream and Mozart. I sit there relishing the experience, the cello solo taming my guilt for abandoning my brothers to their energetic dish washing for the sake of making a hasty exit.

As close as I can figure it, this tendency has a history, going back to the days when Trappists were ascetic to the extreme. Hair-shirts and self-flagellation went hand in hand with a life of ongoing penance, part of which involved consumption of slight quantities of tasteless food as if a sin. By the same reasoning, such things as poetry, art, and music were discouraged, barely tolerating Gregorian chant during liturgy. A twelfth-century monk expressed this logic as suffering in this life so as to avoid suffering in the life to come. Vatican II helped Trappists soften this world-denying tendency by viewing contemplation not as a denial but as an affirmation, losing one's self in the richly divine depths of each "now" as a loving gift.

Many folks today would look askance on this vestige of asceticism at our monastic meals, but actually it resembles the way many Americans live today. "Fast food" has become a way of life—from MacDonald's to TV dinners, from eating on the run to morning coffee with one-handed driving. Savoring a family meal together has almost become an endangered species. There is sadness in any lifestyle that encourages acceleration through life, missing the treasure of the deep moments that give spice to the meaning of the whole. American life is shriveling value into utility, quality into quantity, creativity into efficiency—assessing time by the measure of money.

This is a powerful reason why the world needs the church—as a modeled reminder, over and over again, that time is for savoring, life is for living, and faith is for its own deep sake. Thus, as we have observed, while secular society flattens its Christmas savoring by packing up after opening presents and a meal, the church is only beginning—intent on savoring for twelve days the fullness of the incarnation gifting us everywhere. While many in our society settle for giving Easter baskets to the children, a new tie for Dad, and a ham dinner from Mom, Christians have barely started their fifty days of Easter resurrecting. What an extended Mardi Gras!

But if the church sanctifies quality over quantity, what is this savoring like? Acts describes it as "being filled with joy." In fact, joy is one of the most frequently used New Testament words. The Easter psalms herald the season as a time for the glad heart to abide in thankful confidence. Indicative is the repetitive greeting by the resurrected Jesus in commencing each encounter with the disciples: "Peace be with you" (John 20:19 RSV). Paul promises that in having been companions with him in suffering you will share his overflowing happiness (2 Cor 1:5 RSV). Whether Christmas or Easter, these are the extended seasons of life-tasting joy, confidence, peace—as intense rehearsals for living the many weeks of Ordinary Time with a smiling soul, an unflappable poise, and a hopeful spirit, glued together with an awesome depth of serenity.

The church has been serious about its happiness, in the past having forbidden us to fast during Eastertide, and even going so far as to prohibit the discomfort of kneeling on Sundays, for they are to be celebrated as "little Easters." Furthermore, Christianity has turned on end our way of reckoning time. While Judaism identifies the day as beginning with sunset, Christians regards each day as beginning with daybreak as harbinger of an ongoing resurrection. Why not, for Christians are to live Eastertide as a delicious warning to the world that Jesus is on the loose.

64. THE JOY CALLED EASTER

I was brought up on the idea that a Christian is a person who imitates Jesus. Since in our Sunday School handouts Jesus was always smiling, especially at children, that seemed like a good way to live. My favorite picture had him knocking gently at the door of one's heart, super polite in never entering without an invitation, his knock never loud enough to annoy the neighbors. I hadn't a clue back then as to the seriousness involved in following the Jesus of Scripture, not yet recognizing him as the one who prefers kicking in our back doors.

It isn't as though the church hadn't provided warnings. As we have already noted, the successive days following Christmas are marked by Stephen the first martyr, then the death of "the beloved disciple," followed by the slaughter of the innocent children by Herod because of Jesus, and finally the martyrdom of Archbishop Thomas Becket. Furthermore, the post-Easter lectionary readings extend this relentless portraiture of martyrdom even to those who dared even mention the name of Jesus. With amazing quickness the early Christians were despised, beaten, tortured, imprisoned, and murdered. So intense was this hatred that within a few years of the crucifixion a man named Saul acquired from authorities his own Patriot Act, justifying breaking into the homes of Christians, dragging even children into the streets for persecution and death.

Yet there is an intriguing irony in all these portraits. In each case the followers of Jesus were characterized by joy. With joy, Peter and John preached daily in the temple, knowing full well that at very least they would be arrested, beaten, and imprisoned. And so they were—flogged and finally released with death threats if ever again they would preach. But they left "full of joy that they had been judged worthy of ill treatment for the sake of the Name" (Acts 5:41 NAB). Joy! This same word keeps being used, as in describing the expression on Stephen's face as stones pummel his body. And during the "great persecution" that followed, everywhere that disciples ministered "there was great joy in that city" (Acts 8:8 NRSV). An alternative translation insists that "the rejoicing in that town rose to fever pitch" (Acts 8:8 NAB). When followers were rejected in Antioch, they shook the dust from their feet "with joy." Appropriate is the responsorial psalm accompanying such lectionary readings that call out for "all the earth to cry out to God with joy." Our Easter hymn at the monastery is just a tab more subdued, using singing of "sober joy."

Strangely, however, we almost never hear the word "joy" in today's secular world. When greeting a checkout clerk with a "How are you?" never would I dream of hearing as response, "I am joyous!" Yet this word saturates not only the New Testament but the church's worship life as well. At Christmas we sing "Joy to the World the Lord Has Come." At Easter the sung words are, "Joy we have who sees Him rise." Joy captures the spirit of Christmas Eve candlelight services, the triumphant atmosphere of Easter Vigil, and the tenor of Easter sunrise services overlooking a tranquil lake. To be sure that we get the message, Eastertide liturgies call for double alleluias.

But is it really possible to maintain such an emotional high for forty Easter days? In reality, after the Holy Week liturgies most pastors I know are ready for a vacation, or at least several elongated naps. Therefore I am coming to realize that joy is not so much an emotion to be retained as it is a

II. LIVING THE SEASONS

"resurrection attitude" to be acquired—through practice. Each of us knows at least several Christians who radiate an upbeat stance toward life, oblivious to either side of the half-empty/half full equation. These are the Easter folk, reborn so as to discern resurrection aching to happen everywhere. For eyes opened to see, redbud trees reapply each spring to be understudies for the role of Moses's burning bush. The ecstasy of playing children distills the rumor of angels. Hugs are novice masters in the formation of love. Pancakes at sunrise are the aroma of new beginnings. Crocuses defying the snow crust qualify as silent theologians. Easter faith is the prism by which to experience Paul's insistence that "with Jesus, the word is never 'No' but always 'Yes.'" The best witness that "Christ is raised" is this kind of joy in which Easter folk testify with their living that Easter is an ongoing happening.

65. EASTER PEACE

My spiritual director is a hermit living high in the Ozark Mountains. Beginning each day at 1:30 AM, his intent is to live every moment fully in the presence of God. Early on in our relationship my question to him was probably as cynical as it was urgent. "How on earth do you know that you are in God's presence?" His answer was as prompt as it was clear—"a deep sense of peace." I cherish still those five words for not only did they identify the underbelly of my own spiritual searchings, but provided a clue for understanding all of us.

Millions of people seek therapeutic help precisely because they cannot find peace—not only in what they do but, more deeply, in who they are. Most external conflicts originate in the absence of internal peace. And while this restless craving for peace is at the heart of being human, most of us look for it lethally in the wrong places. "Spirituality" is the present-day code word for those more conscious of their searching for peace—and it has something to do with Easter.

As we noted, almost every time the resurrected Christ appears to his disciples, his greeting is "Peace be with you" (John 20:19 RSV). Our eucharistic liturgies echo this Easter promise. "Deliver us, Lord, from every evil, and grant us peace in our day." And again: "Lord Jesus Christ, you said to your apostles, I leave you peace, my peace I give you." To these words is added the act of offering each other "the sign of peace." Our benedictions offer the same blessing: May "the Lord lift up his countenance upon you, and give you peace" (Num 6:26 RSV). And again: "Now may the God of peace..." (Heb 13:20). And still again: "The peace of God, which passes all understanding, will keep yours hearts and your minds in Christ Jesus" (Phil 4:7 RSV).

Not surprisingly, then, we find peace to be the centering mind-set of the early Christians. The peace of Christ is mentioned ninety-one times in the New Testament. Prior to Easter, the disciples are portrayed as coarse, uneducated, unsophisticated, awkward, and naïve—quickly frightened, often confused, and self-interested to the point of abandonment and betrayal. After Easter, however, the portrait is amazingly reversed. These bewildered and despairing disciples have become so centered in an inexplicable peace that they dare to stand eagerly before the educated and powerful elites of their time, courageously unflappable unto death. Stephen as the first martyr was so gifted with this undergirding peace that in witnessing for Christ even his foes "saw that his face was like the face of an angel" (Acts 6:15 RSV). And as he was being stoned, this defining peace was so profound that he resembled Jesus himself, praying that his killers be forgiven. Even more, he was able to commend his spirit with the very words of Jesus (Acts 7:59–60 RSV).

Relatedly, monks close each day by chanting the words of Simeon: "Lord, now let your servant go in peace . . . ." The accompanying blessing ends, ". . . that awake, we may keep watch with Christ, and asleep, rest in his peace." Sprinkled with water as a reminder of our baptism into Christ's death and resurrection, we enter the Great Silence with this blessing: "May the all-powerful Lord grant us a restful night and a peaceful death." The word of words, then, is "peace"—and Easter is Christ's rejoinder to this deep craving in each of us. Resurrection is from the inside out, arising as a calm invincibility, a tranquil stillness, a Teflon soul, a quiet contentment, a rare poise, and a trusting serenity no matter what. Peace is the Easter name for the resurrection gift of trusting that nothing "will be able to separate us from the love of God in Christ Jesus our Lord" (Rom 8:39 RSV). He is risen. Indeed.

66. EASTER FEAR

Strange though it sounds, fear is what the disciples experience on the evening of the day when they begin to hear rumors of resurrection. As with many of us, their modicum of faith has much to do with fear. They lock the doors and windows of the upper room, purportedly in fear of the authorities. But deeper than fright for their lives is a fear issuing from a deep sense of guilt. They are huddled together in deep remorse not only for what they have done to Jesus, but even more, for what they had failed to do.

My mother used a one-liner for "putting the fear of God" in me: "Just wait until your father gets home!" It carried over into my fledgling faith—for if God was like my father that she portrayed as "coming soon," that's fear! So if rumors about resurrection would actually turn out to be true, the situation the disciples fantasized about was one of strongly mixed emotions. When Jesus had needed them most, that was precisely when they had abandoned him, betrayed him, and denied him. "Just wait until . . . !" No wonder the word "terrified" was used to describe the disciples at the empty tomb, and "frightened" because of "fear" is the expressed mood in the upper room (Luke 24:4 RSV and John 20:19 RSV).

These are the mixed emotions, then, that prepare us to participate in the drama about to unfold. In spite of all locked door precautions, "Jesus himself stood among them." Yes indeed, most certainly, "they were startled and frightened" (Luke 24:36 RSV). This is the moment when we can understand the incredible power of the reversal that occurs with the four-word greeting by Jesus: "Peace be with you." So utterly unexpected are such words that Jesus has to repeat them (John 20:19, 21 RSV). They are stunned. But there is no anger, no guilt-tripping, no imposition of shame—none! Instead, the words are amazingly gentle: "I am with you." That is all they need to hear. What is most unbelievable about this narrative is not Jesus' Houdini act with locked doors, but the unlocking of the disciples' fear—for they are being amazingly embraced as forgiven friends. Miraculously, he is still their divine companion, and they know now that he will remain so, no matter what. "Do not be afraid; go and tell . . . " (Matt 28:10 RSV). Indeed, as they grabbed their walking sticks and headed for the nearest bus station to Galilee. We can understand, then, why in telling of the resurrection enthusiastically "to all nations," their preaching was of "repentance and forgiveness" (Luke 24:47 RSV).

67. RESURRECTION OF THE SMALL

One might be surprised to learn that resurrection for Paul is something that occurs not just once but over and over—and at its heart is not so much what happens on the outside but inside each Christian (Rom 6:3f RSV). This is why he favors baptism by immersion, for it dramatizes that in being plunged three times into water we are participating in Christ's three days in the tomb, and thus raised with Christ into a cleansed newness of resurrected life. Baptism is our personal Easter. In the early church this involved being renamed, usually for a martyr, for martyrs were the ones whose baptism into Christ's death was near literal. "We were buried therefore with him by baptism into death, so that as Christ was raised from the death by the glory of the Father, we too might walk in newness of life" (Rom 6:4 RSV). The old is drowned in forgiveness, and the new arises as Christ dies our death for us.

That is true freedom. Yet, amazingly, Easter involves more. Almost every scriptural account of Jesus' resurrection appearance occurs "when they were at table." Luke testifies that all who were "witnesses" of the resurrection were those "who ate and drank with him after he rose from the death" (Acts 10:41 RSV). The resurrection occurs as eyes are opened "in the breaking of the bread" (Luke 24:35 RSV). "Real Presence" is the church's historic way of saying that the Eucharist is a table of reoccurring resurrection. On the altar is unfolded a linen napkin called a "corporal" ("body") that symbolizes "the napkin which had been on his head." And on it are placed the bread and wine to be resurrected for and in us as his body and blood (John 20:7 RSV). This "presence" is our recurrent Easter.

But there is still more. Resurrection does not mean that some impersonal spark in us continues on after death. Resurrection involves the very personhood of Jesus, and thus its promise touches our personalities as well—the very heart of what makes each of us special. Easter is big because of its implications for the small. In preaching this theme in an Easter sermon at the monastery, I directed this promise to each monk by name, recalling explicitly some of the delightful uniquenesses of each that I would want wrapped in their resurrection promise. My reminiscences ranged the gamut—lover of Bach, connoisseur of pea soup, proprietor of a mischievous smile, teller of dumb jokes, trimmer of roses, shy writer of poetry, gifted listener, daffodil planter, planer of cedar. My testimony was that the Easter promise deals with the biggies—the gifts of forgiveness and real presence. But equally important, the Easter promise embraces the very small—those little things that matter so much about each of us. God's resurrection memory is a promise about remembering, eager to retell the stories with us.

II. LIVING THE SEASONS

68. WHAT'S IN A NAME?

I have shared how the events of Scripture can be understood in terms of the old movie theatre gimmick that kept us kids coming back, whetting our appetites and loosening our pockets. I still remember a Batman serial episode entitled "Robin, Boy Wonder, Doomed to Die." Here he is, tied to the base of a gigantic wine press, as The Penguin, with sinister laughter, slowly brings the piston down to crush our hero. But wait, Batman is calling out, "Robin!" [CUT] I shall always feel a little deprived because the next week I got sick and never got to see what happened. But Batman did call.

It wouldn't take an accomplished film director to create the same effect with the scriptural portrait of Mary Magdalene waiting at the tomb. We could entitle it, "Mary, the First to Experience, and Tell All." The first episode could end quoting Scripture: "The disciples went back to their homes . . . ." [CUT] That's enough of a teaser to hint that there is more, because if the resurrected Christ ever encounters you, you can't go home again. In the next episode, Mary, knowing that she no longer has a home, is waiting with tears, just waiting, not knowing for what. "It is all in the waiting," says T. S. Eliot. [CUT] The music rises, the sound of "maybe"—yes, but she doesn't recognize him by sight. [CUT] Then the final episode, when he calls her by name, and the recognition is instant. "Mary." "Rabboni!" [END] That's it, for this is what makes Easter *Easter*. The "more" for which she was waiting was to hear her name. What's in a name? The heart of resurrection.

The most powerful word for me in the whole English language is "Paul." If you want something from me, just use that magic word. When I answer the telephone and the voice asks for "Mr. Jones" or "Dr. Jones," I am strongly tempted to hang up. They do not know me. But if the voice says, "Paul, is that you?," they have my full attention. At the evening service of Compline, the monks chant this verse: "Since he clings to me in love I will free him, protect him for he knows my name" (Ps 91:14 Grail). Isaiah understands this power of calling by name, making it a central act of God: "I have called you by name, you are mine" (Isa 43:1 RSV). And again, "Upon the palms of my hands I have written your name" (Isa 49:16 NAB). Last week a friend sent me words from a hymn he had found. "Will you love the 'you' you hide if I call your name?" When Jesus called "Saul," it was a newly named "Paul" who emerged.

During an Easter sermon at the monastery, I used this idea of resurrection through name calling, suggesting that we were in this place because each of us had heard the calling of our name. I went around the stalls, calling out to each monk the only word he ever needed to hear: "Theodore . . . Christopher . . . ." Afterwards the Abbot said to me, "That was gutsy. I couldn't do it, because I'd be afraid I would forget someone's name." "Well," I responded, "guess that's the heart of the Easter good news. Christ never forgets anyone's name." It seems that he etches them with Good Friday blood on his Easter heart.

69. KILLERS AT EASTER

Some years ago a parishioner cornered me one Sunday with angry tears. "I'm sick and tired not only of your stand against the death penalty, but this morning you even prayed for those on death row. I almost walked out. By affirming killers you denigrate the horrible sufferings of their victims and families." She had a point. She didn't know about my work in organizing support groups for victims' families. So I asked for her forgiveness for what sounded like a narrow compassion—and asked if she would have coffee with me. She agreed, but little coffee was drunk. It became a time for shared tears. She shared about a close relative who had been violently killed by a robber. I shared about how my friend Ruth had stopped one night when someone waved her down in apparent need of help—only to be pulled from her car, raped, and choked to death. "Have you forgiven him?" she asked. "I'm trying," I said. Together we recalled how the Pope had gone to the cell of his attempted assailant and offered forgiveness.

Jesus has a way of messing with persons. Not only does he say, "Do not let your heart be trouble," but he lived it. Even as nails were being driven into his hands and feet, he looked straight into the eyes of his tormentors who would soon be his murderers. Not only did he speak words of forgiveness but he made excuses for them. For many years, now, I have been working to abolish the death penalty in Missouri, making "life without parole" the maximum sentence. This seems a reasonable and doable request. But to forgive Ruth's murderer who shows no signs of remorse and apparently has no interest in forgiveness? This is the time when it is easier to stay in Good Friday—harboring the anger, feeling the darkness, and nursing the pain. To push on through into Easter, that's tough. Believing that Jesus rose from the dead is a lot easier than living the resurrection. Jesus' way of doing it was "not my will but thine be done." And God's will here is clear: "I came not to condemn . . . ." And again, "Though your sins be as scarlet . . . ." And again, "Love your enemy . . . ." And again, "You have heard it said, 'An eye

II. LIVING THE SEASONS

for an eye . . .' but I say to you . . . ." Resurrection means bringing new life out of dead ends.

"An eye for an eye" stuff can get nasty, with illustrations amply available—all the way from grade school playground skirmishes to out-and-out warfare. Smashing someone's cheek rather than turning one's own brings only an escalating anger for revenge. But how is it possible to live the alternative, really? The process Jesus proposes is clear enough: "Let the one without sin cast the first stone"—or pull the switch, or do the lethal injecting. I speak with each person in Missouri the night of his execution, either in person or by telephone. It is usually with tears. I sometimes invite a vigorous supporter of the death penalty to do the same, for to affirm killing in absentia is very different from telling a human voice that they deserve to be exterminated.

For Jesus, sin goes far deeper than actual acts, all the way into our desires: "He who lusts in his heart has already . . . ." Easter conversion occurs at heart level or not at all, after tasting a Good Friday condemnation. In the words of Ahab, "Have you found me out . . . ?" "Yes" (1 Kgs 21:20 RSV). Condemning others is our favorite way of blinding ourselves to the seamy desires seeping out around the edges, even of our non-actions. Our professed innocence is most often simply a lack of opportunity. "Damn you!" is an angry disclosure of desire. Yes, "there but for the grace of God go I." So exposed and humbled, the implications become clear. The ability to forgive resides in our first having experienced a forgiveness that is undeserved. Happy Easter.

70. MOTHER'S DAY AND THE DAYS AFTER

There is a particular scriptural image of God that gives me trouble, even though it appears often. Take the story of the scribe going through the land marking the foreheads of the few persons who are to be spared, as God shrieks out for the soldiers of Israel to murder all the rest. Even old men, youth and maidens, women and children—wipe them all out; screams God! You shall show no pity (Ezek 9:1–11 NRSV). The psalmist reinforces this portrait of God as the one who flays the nations with a rod of iron, to "dash them in pieces like a potter's vessel" (Ps 2:9 RSV). The book of Revelation continues this imagery in declaring that the Son whom Mary has birthed, the one whom we thought to be the Prince of Peace, "is to rule all the nations with a rod of iron" (Rev 12:5 RSV). He possesses a "sharp sword with which to smite the nation . . . , and he will tread the wine press of the fury of the wrath of God the Almighty" (Rev 19:15 RSV).

I cringe before such portraits, not in fear but in loathing—especially when various political leaders today are executing horrendous acts of violence in the name of some such God. And ironically, many of the persons picked for violation and slaughter are those who themselves are committed to a God. The Rule of Saint Benedict declares that the first step in attained unity with God is to have the fear of God always before your eyes, for God watches always what is inside and what is out, and his angels report daily. So much for having a "guardian angel." He's a snitch.

I find solace in Julian of Norwich's insistence that there can be no anger in God for if there were, even for a minute, the universe would no longer be. What these violent images force us as Christians to do is stop seizing on Scripture with dogged literalism—and instead screen all of our images of God through the lens that is Jesus Christ. Paul is right, that in Scripture "we have this treasure in earthen vessels," a revelation humanly received by those whose with their own tainted perspectives (2 Cor 4:7 RSV). Because we believe that Jesus is the ultimate disclosure of the God whose soul is love, we must suspect as unduly earthen any characteristics assigned to God that do not pass this test.

So as we males continue to wage competitively our macho carnage in war after war, who is it that holds things together through it all? It is the mothers—those who suckle the infants, rummage through rubbish to feed the elderly, and model gentleness by embracing their children against the faces and instruments of hatred. This may be why many of us find so appealing the portraits of Madonna and Child. In a profound sense, Christianity is a women's thing, a mother thing—on behalf of all humanity. Mary's own portrait of God is the one who "has put down the mighty from their thrones, and exalts those of low degree," compassionately seeing that the hungry "are filled with good things" (Luke 1:52 RSV). Although we men are inclined to overlook them, feminine images for God do appear in Scripture and they are powerful. God is like a woman in labor (Isa 42:24 RSV), carrying us in the womb and giving birth to us (Isa 46:3 RSV), betrayed like a wife forsaken (Isa 54:6 RSV), yet showing us a mother's comfort (Isa 66:13 RSV), ministering to us as "a nurse carries a sucking child" (Num 11:12 RSV), relating to us as a husband who loves his spouse (Hos 2:16–20 RSV), keeping us "safe upon mother's breast" (Ps 22:9 RSV)—climaxing in a Jesus who yearns to gather us all unto himself "as a hen gathers her brood under her wings" (Luke 13:34 RSV).

Mondays were hard for me as a child, trudging off to school "the day after" a weekend of playful freedom. Yet my mother was there at the door with a departing hug, and was waiting with a kiss when I returned home, dirty or not. If I got sick at school, I could trust that she would soon be there. What a fine image for God—trusting that on every "day after" God will be there, in our comings and goings, waiting and ready to embrace the household of the world.

That is what Mother's Day is to be about. In 1872 Julia Ward Howe established it as an antiwar observance, celebrating women's sensitivity to nonviolence and to nurturing. In contrast to the image of a scribe identifying with Magic Marker the few who are to escape a murderous God, let us temper our imagery with the portrait of a "Mother God" marking foreheads with a kiss that promises always to be there. Thanks, Mom, on this your day.

71. SUCKER-STICK ASCENSION

It may come as a surprise that while ascension is largely passed over by many denominations, the church historically has regarded it as central. I admit that if taken literally it is one of those biblical events best forgotten. How are we to believe in our scientific age that a person can defy gravity, lifting off like a balloon? And how could he breathe without a space suit? And where would he go, given that the Hubble telescope has checked out space for light-years upon light-years, and there is no observable heaven to which he could have ascended?

Thus we Christians need to ask on this Ascension Day, as we need quite often to ask at other times, not "could he" but "what difference would it make?" This question needs to be asked wherever literalism threatens to render problematic some part of our faith. Christmas can flounder over what to make of a woman who becomes pregnant without having sex. Easter can falter over a dead man getting up and walking around. In such scenarios, the deepest question to ask is, "Whether literally true or false, so what?" If literally true, such "miracles" might deserve front billing on the evening news, shifting public attention away from the latest celebrity scandal. But the next morning, what lasting significance remains? That is the question to be addressed to the ascension.

Ascension correlates directly to how we understand the incarnation. God did not enter our human realm for only thirty-some years, returning unchanged to wherever and however he was before. Since the Christ event is the disclosure of God's very nature, this means that God is incarnate from the beginning of the world. That is who God is, even though before the Jesus event it may have been only dimly suspected. Meister Eckhart put this well. "From all eternity God lies on a maternity bed giving birth. The essence of God is birthing." Thus Christmas is always and forever. "Flesh" is not what God put on once, like a garment, and then took off, throwing it in a corner as if a bloodstained jumpsuit. It is what God ongoingly assumes for that is who God by nature is.

Ascension, then, is the celebration of the incarnation's amazing implications. What God takes up into himself is not the disembodied spirit of Jesus. Tradition insists that the risen Christ retains even the cruel marks of his crucified humanness. This symbolism is powerful—that the one "sitting at the right hand of the Father" does so with perforated hands, pierced side, and bloody brow. As the hymn expresses it, "In human shape and flesh adorned, with his Passion's scars he ascended." Or another hymn: "Christ our fellow sufferer, yet retains a fellow feeling of our pains, and still remembers in the skies, his tears, agonies, cries." Ascension is the celebration of an astonishing God who is ongoingly incarnate, ongoingly resurrecting, and ongoingly ascending—as the joys, sorrows, tears, and dreams of our personal and corporate histories become part of God's ongoing pilgrimage in becoming all in all. Leo the Great agrees, that "Christ has not abandoned us when he ascended, but takes our very humanity with him." The bleeding Christ ascends into the Godhead, as our living becomes ingredient to God's own pilgrimage. Abhishiktanda underscores this: "Christ's ascent towards the fullness of communion with the Father is one with the ascent of humanity itself, of the universe, towards the final koinonia which is the mystery of the church" [*Prayer* (Philadelphia: Westminster, 1967, p. 12].

The difference that the doctrine of Ascension makes, then, is that it speaks directly to our lives in particular and to history as a whole. How tragic if our pain, struggles, hopes, and dreams are all in vain, having no lasting part in the larger scheme of things. Ascension is the marvelous promise that God is weaving into the fabric of his kingdom the precious threads of each life, in a design so intricate that it will include even the act of an autistic child propping up with a sucker stick the trampled face of a dandelion. Thus Jesus' instruction to his disciples has a deeper than literal meaning: "Gather up the fragments left over, that nothing may be lost" (John 6:12 RSV).

72. PENTECOST AND INTERTWINING LITURGY

An exciting feature of the church's liturgy is the way in which different celebrations can interweave creatively. We have noted how Paul intersects baptism with Holy Week in being our participation in Christ's death and resurrection. So it is that the meaning of Pentecost can be intensified through its own brand of intertwining. The triad of Lent-Easter-Pentecost has its parallel in the triad of Advent-Christmas-Epiphany—both making concrete the divine dynamic of promise, fulfillment, and response. Since Pentecost and Epiphany are both our "responses" to God's primary acts, it is natural that they commingle. At Epiphany, the Magi depart from the Christmas manger to spread the good news throughout the world. At Pentecost this call becomes personalized in each of us. Thirty years after the Magi begin their mission, the resurrected Jesus instructs his followers to "go therefore and make disciples of all nations" (Matt 28:19 RSV). And yet he "charged them not to depart from Jerusalem, but to wait." They need first to "be baptized with the Holy Spirit" (Acts 1:4–5 RSV). Through our Pentecostal baptism we are all empowered to become the Wise Ones, called to universalize the evangelization begun with Epiphany.

Imagination, in turn, invites us to recognize how Pentecost intertwines with Christmas. Mary is the first to experience Pentecost, for "the Holy Spirit will come upon you and the power of the Most High will overshadow you" (Luke 1:35 RSV). And Mary, in turn, being the first to believe the good news, models for us our personal Pentecost—in which we become mangers for Christ's birth, as we too are "filled with the Holy Spirit" (Acts 2:4 RSV). The incarnation that occurred in Mary is the incarnation that Pentecost continues in us. St. Paul expresses this intermingling as a rhetorical question: "Do you not know that you are God's temple and that God's Spirit dwells in you?" (1 Cor 3:16 RSV).

Furthermore, Pentecost becomes Christmas for the church. At her birthday, the church becomes the manger, birthing it as the "body of Christ." Likewise our imaginations ignite intersections of Pentecost with Easter. Paul again leads the way. "If the Spirit of him who raised Jesus from the dead dwells in you, he who raised Christ Jesus from the dead will give life to your mortal bodies also through his Spirit which dwells in you" (Rom 8:11 RSV). Dead to our old bodies and rising as new selves, Pentecost becomes our Happy Easter—and Merry Christmas. The reasons for the seasons interweave—gifting us with the richest of tapestries. Let the Christian without imagination cast the first literal stone.

73. PENTECOST AND ASCENSION FEAR

The church's drama at Easter Vigil begins by lighting a huge Easter candle that symbolizes Christ as the risen light of the world. This candle leads the procession into the darkened church, remembered as having been totally stripped on Good Friday. This candle remains as a lighted focus for the services throughout the forty days of Easter joy. Therefore what puzzles me is that while tradition understandably called for extinguishing the Easter candle on Ascension Sunday, why do many church liturgies today now call for the candle to remain lighted until Pentecost Sunday, a week later? This change might seem trivial, but it reflects a theological difference worth our attention. Good liturgy makes for excellent drama—as the acting out of spoken meaning. Therefore wouldn't the impact of ascension be better served if with the scriptural words "he parted from them," the Easter candle would be extinguished? Poof, doused, snuffed out, smothered, quenched, gone, dark! This would dramatize the beginning of a deeply pensive week. But if, instead, we permit the candle to remain lighted, it can convey a suspicion that the church is afraid to undergo the plight belonging to everyone without the gift of the Comforter—an absence taunting our society as emptiness, abandonment, loneliness, and a fear of silence.

After Ascension Day should come a darkened week, parallel to the disheartening experience of Holy Saturday. Abandoned by death then, we are haunted by absence now. On both days we might be tempted to pray, "Our Nada who art in Nada, Nada be thy name." Our one day of Holy Saturday is insufficient, for we are immediately rushed into its Easter erasure. Honesty about life requires a bottomless sense of anxiety over abandonment. So at least for the darkened week between Ascension departure and Pentecostal descent, let us sense the fingers of panic over our possible cosmic aloneness.

Put another way, hide though we try, we cannot escape the sadness of separations. There is the empty house as a child toddles off to kindergarten; a memory bedroom after a teenager leaves for college; the bittersweet marriage of a son or daughter; a spouse abandoned to loneliness through divorce or death; moving a parent into a nursing home. How appropriate it would be, then, that our post-ascension week be a time for immersion together in this forlorn disposition of life, exacerbated by deprivation of even the divine presence. Ascension would signal that from this point on, being a Christian is based not on sight but on the gamble of faith alone. "Faith is the assurance of things hoped for, the conviction of things not seen" (Heb 11:1 RSV). The Christ event is God's engagement to humanity, promising marriage for richer or poorer and sickness or health, the whole bit. *But he left us*, leaving only a promise of return, sometime or other—a scribbled IOU. Scripture identifies how much at this point we are like believers before Christ—all of whom "died in faith, not having received what was promised" (Heb 11:13 RSV).

The martyr Oscar Romero declared that only the truly poor can celebrate Christian for they are the ones "who know they need someone to come on their behalf." So it is that Easter has little meaning without a pungent taste of Good Friday's finality in death. The raised chalice at Holy Communion is trivial unless we have drunk to its dregs a cup of another kind. And now here, without this week of separation we are unlikely to grasp the incredible gift that is Pentecost. Without having previously experienced the forlorn experience of having been left, Pentecost is likely to be little more than the story of a weird phenomenon. Without remembering the empty nest syndrome, the missing, the yearning, the homesickness, we are prone to take for granted God's everlasting embrace as the Holy Spirit. Love is tasted at its deepest level when it is a homecoming, a reunion, after a lonely absence.

So let us blow out our Easter candle at Ascension, leaving us dimly with only Jesus's short cryptic promise: "I will not leave you desolate; I will come to you" (John 14:18 RSV). But when? Reminiscent is one's feelings on hearing the lover sing in the ballad: "I'm leaving on a jet plane, I don't know when I'll be back again." Actually, in having only this thread of hope, our faith can be purified—in trusting Christ as the one who not only makes but keeps promises. With a smoldering wick, we can be retaught the art of waiting, holding on to a remembrance of the one who is worth waiting for.

74. PERSISTENT FLAME—A SECOND THOUGHT

Having fussed about the symbolism of extinguishing the Easter candle on Ascension Sunday, I confess that there is a way of finding meaning if we do keep it lit. Some of us felt a strange tug in first hearing the motel commercial promising to "leave the light on for you." There are "widow walks" on the top of old seaport homes in New England where a woman would light a lantern and watch, refusing to give up hope that her sailor lover would still return. So if the church keeps the Easter candle lighted after the Ascension departure, let it be a liturgical expression of love-sickness, leaving the flame faithfully lighted in hope of our lover's return. Then Pentecost can be "the rush of a mighty wind" that blows out our tiny widowed candle, unneeded for the Christ-sailor has been strangely blown back to harbor. The Pentecostal return, then, can be understood as the consummation of the promised divine-human marriage. The Holy Spirit weds our souls, moving in with us to establish a home. The incarnational promise has become the Pentecostal fact, for we left a light on for him.

75. PENTECOST AS EASTER

Pentecost can be understood as a name for our personal Holy Week. After the portrayal of Pentecost in John's gospel, the resurrected Jesus shows the disciples his own wounds before sending them forth: "As the father has sent me, so I send you" (John 20:21 RSV). This means that the Spirit that is Pentecost sends us out like Jesus was sent, to face Good Friday woundedness—hands, feet, pride, foes, and reputation. Yet the specialness of our Pentecost is that we are not sent out alone. The Holy Spirit is our promised companion—with us and in us and for us. By being "filled with the Holy Spirit," Peter and we are emboldened to confront leaders with the courageous insistence that "the stone rejected by you, the builders ... has become the cornerstone" (Acts 4:11 NAB). Because the despised one has become our pearl of great price, everything is being turned upside down. This is our resurrection—when the impossible becomes possible, the first is to be last, the enemy is embraced as friend, the stranger is welcomed as buddy, the meek will inherit the earth, and the dead shall live forever. This Pentecostal resurrection entails for us a conversion of lifestyle, in which society's working values are exposed for us as temptations to sin.

A telling mark of our pentecostal Holy Week is the spontaneous change of pronouns. The unredeemed human condition is marked by an obsession with "I," "me," and "mine." Even if we do not declare this publicly, inside the voices whisper, "nobody's going to tell me what to do," "I never get the recognition I deserve," "what's in it for me?" These are expressions of the self's lower frontier. The pentecostal change involves an exchange of

II. LIVING THE SEASONS

pronouns. The Christian's grammar favors "we," "us," and "our." While life was formerly a personal game, the agenda now is one of common endeavor. Poverty, unemployment, human rights—these are resurrected now as *our* issues, for "*we* the people."

The first Pentecost birthed a new reality called the church, a community characterized above all by its radical contrast to the selfishness defining "this crooked generation." The driving motivation was in having "one heart and soul," so communal that they regarded as sinful whatever was privately clutched. Christians were understood as stewards, called to share "everything in common" so that "there was not a needy person among them" (Acts 4:32, 34 RSV). What these early Christians were coming to grasp was that the depth of faith is to be measured by the size of the circumference defining their "we." Conversion probably began for them, as for us, with an intensification of love toward family, then friends, followed hesitantly toward one's associates, no matter how much they might try one's patience. But this was to be only the beginning, for the depth of Christian maturation is measured by how expansive the Spirit-driven inclusiveness. The practice field for the "we" was one's congregation, including every member without exception. Then the expansion bubbled over externally into an inclusivity that embraced the neighborhood. And then? Foreigners? Government? Illegal immigrants? The imprisoned? Death row? Ethnics? Gay folks? And then? Beyond society and nation to include Iran? Russia? What about terrorists?

It is not hard to see where Jesus is taking them, and us. The inclusivity of the Christian circle is to be total, absolutely so, without any exception whatsoever. How could it be otherwise, for our God is the Creator who has the whole world in his hands, the Redeemer who continues to suffer the sins of the whole world into forgiveness, and the Holy Spirit who is knocking on the door of every heart?

Put succinctly, the Good Friday-Easter-Ascensional-Pentecostal lifestyle involves the expansiveness of loving as we are being loved. Conversion involves being astounded by the breadth and length and height and depth of this sacrificial love by Christ, especially for us who are so undeserving of it. Embraced within the circle of such loving, there is no one, no where, no time, for any reason, who is to be excluded. Christians are to grant no person or any group the right to be our enemy, for whatever exclusive diameter they might draw, the horizon of the Christian circle is always drawn so as to include them. It is indicative, then, that the original Pentecost embraced representatives from all fifteen nations of the known world, each telling in their "own native language" the mighty works of God in inclusive resurrection (Acts 2:8 NAB).

76. PENTECOST DIVERSITY

Scripture portrays two contrasting ways in which Pentecost happened and can happen—then and now. The Acts of the Apostles provides the *extrovert* version. "They were all gathered together in one place. And suddenly a sound came from heaven like the rush of a mighty wind"—complete with "tongues as of fire" (Acts 2:1–2 RSV). Joyous, interactive, communal, recalling the hymn, "Hail Thee, Festival Day"—"swiftly descend," "sevenfold." John's gospel, on the other hand, provides the *introvert* scenario. The scene is the intimate upper room on Easter evening, and there Jesus "breathed on them, and said to them, 'Receive the Holy Spirit'" (John 20:22 RSV). Simple, gentle, close, quiet, recalling the hymn, "Breathe on me, Breath of God, fill me with life anew."

Instead of being disturbed by these contrasting scriptural versions of Pentecost, we should welcome this diversity. The Bible is composed of various books written from diverse perspectives, giving key events a rich tapestry of meanings. This diversity correlates well with the contrasting ways in which persons perceive and process common experiences. The Myers-Briggs Personality Inventory illustrates this well. The extrovert, feeling, sensing, judging personality type will likely identify with the Acts description of Pentecost. These are the folk who know firsthand how lives can be shaken by strong winds so as to evoke responses that are often emotional, public, and sometimes boisterous. Alcoholics Anonymous meetings often provide lively stories of such graphic turnabouts.

An introvert, thinking, intuitive, perceiving type is more likely to identify with John's description, in which knowing the resurrected Christ is more like a whisper confiding, "Peace be with you" (John 20:22 RSV). Like Elijah who does not hear God in the wind and the earthquake, God is heard as "a still small voice" (1 Kgs 19:12 RSV). For these, there is less drama and more inner growth. Instead of baptism being a radical about-face, it consists more of seeds being planted, Eucharist providing the nurturing, confirmation affirming that the seeds have taken root, and Pentecost a strengthening for harvest.

II. LIVING THE SEASONS

Since God creates each of us as unique, we must resist efforts to force one size or type of Christianity on us all. And yet, since we are inimitable, it is likely that the "pentecostal experience" will happen to each of us more than once, with the possibility of variable versions. Thus introverts need not repress or be embarrassed by strange desires to express robust joy for no apparent reason. And extroverts, in turn, should not neglect the precious inner urgings to season their doings with graceful moments of gentle peace. The church is a pentecostal community in which through shared stories we discover the rich anatomy of the Spirit's adventures among us.

77. TRINITY: THREE AS ONE, OR ONE AS THREE?

On the liturgical calendar, Trinity Sunday is the first Sunday after Pentecost. Churches find a way of rendering Ascension Sunday graphic by loosening helium balloons, and celebrating Pentecost with red streamers fastened to everything. But what on earth can one do with Trinity Sunday? While this day commemorates a central Christian doctrine, it is one of the most difficult and misunderstood of doctrines. I wonder if there is anyone in a typical congregation who can say much more than "Trinity means God is three and yet one, whatever that means!" Key questions raised by the idea of Trinity are these: why do we have it, can we conceive it; why is it important; and how can it be lived?

As to the question of *why we have the doctrine*, it resulted from the struggles of the early church to understand who Jesus really is. Some claimed that he was fully human but not fully divine; others understood him as fully divine but not fully human. To this confusion, Athanasius brought clarity through simple logic: if redemption can only be a gift from God, and if it has come to us through the human Jesus, then it follows that he is both. OK, but if Jesus is somehow divine, how does he relate to the God whom he himself called "Father"? To confuse this situation even more, Scripture insists on God as the Holy Spirit who at Pentecost comes to dwell within us. Now what?

Efforts to *conceive* this conundrum start with this question: is the problem primarily how the three can be one, or how the one can be three? The Eastern Church tradition preferred the image of three-as-one. Beginning with Father, Son, and Holy Spirit as scripturally given, the unity of the three can be imaged with the idea of a "Social Trinity." God is social, communal in nature. It follows that since we are created in God's image, we too are created to be social, coming to fullness when as individuals we become one in unity with others, in the church as the divine-human "body of Christ." Yet it is difficult with this imagery of the "Godhead" to avoid a tritheistic picture of three different "persons," as it were, seated on three different thrones.

Western Christendom, on the other hand, has tended to follow Augustine's one-as-three approach. The one God has three essential "manifestations." Since we are created in God's image, we should be able to find analogies of such threeness in our own oneness. This we find by analogy with our mind—composed of intellect, memory, and will, each distinct in operation yet all three are necessary for our oneness.

Tertullian found a helpful analogy in the theatre of his time. By using a different mask (called a "persona") for each character in a drama, one actor could play more than one role. Thus the one God has three "personae," not "persons" as in separate "personalities," but distinguishable "roles." Just as one person can be wife, mother, and teacher, so the Trinity does not mean three separate self-conscious "beings" but one God who functions as Creator, Redeemer, and Inspirer. Paul roots this understanding in his own Christian experience. "It is the God who said 'Let light shine in the darkness' [Creator] who shines in our hearts now [Holy Spirit] to give the light of the knowledge of the glory of God in the face of Christ [Redeemer]" (2 Cor 4:6, own translation).

Third, *why is the Trinity important*? Well, if God is only *Creator*, then we would have "deism," a God who begins the world but has apparently been on vacation ever since. If God is only *Redeemer*, how are we to account for the world's creation and for why it exists? If God is only *Inspirer* working within us, then creation and history are not within God's domain, rendering us solitary sparks within an alien world. Thus the Christian needs a God who relates to us in all three ways. Paul's way of putting this is that God is the One in whom we live (Son), move (Holy Spirit), and have our being (Father).

Finally, *what might it mean to live the Trinity*? A God who is triune provides us with a rich spirituality. Focusing on God as *Creator*, we are drawn into the mystery of all that exists, with reverence for the power that sustains every speck in each moment. The dark hours particularly radiate this mystic awe-struckness—a star-adorned sky, moonlight waltzing among aspen shadows, an unseen brook chanting responses to the whippoorwill call just beyond the breeze. Such experiences of spellbound loss of self elicit what St. Theresa of Avila calls the "prayer of quiet" and Thomas Keating and others teach as "Centering Prayer." There is awe simply in existing.

Focusing on God as *Redeemer*, we are opened to the incarnate companionship of God, as in Br. Lawrence's "practicing the presence." Sharing his monastic job with God, the two of them become co-cooks. He and God are best friends, sharing everything from seasoning the soup to smelling the lilacs outside the kitchen window.

Focusing on God as *Inspirer* invites us into a spirituality of creativity, luring us into becoming midwives with God through our imagination. "Doing God's will" means discerning and birthing in beauty the Spirit's yearnings, being led through opening doors, becoming co-creators in God's becoming all in all.

Trinity, then, is really a one-word summary of the gospel. Ours is a triune God who creates and sustains everything that exists, who out of love for us becomes redemptively incarnate in our history, so that in every "now" we can experience the Spirit as the endless flow of life gifting us with creativity, peace, and joy at soul depth. At our deepest level, we are truly existing in God—the triune One in whom we live, and move, and have our being.

78. VALENTINE JESUS

For Protestants, the "Feast of the Most Sacred Heart of Jesus" is a strangely Catholic thing—commemorating someone's heart! Celebrated on Friday following the second Sunday after Pentecost, the very next day commemorates the "Immaculate Heart of Mary, and these are preceded by "The Most Holy Body and Blood of Christ" on the first Sunday after Trinity. This imagery reflects a time in history when the heart was anatomically regarded as the center of our emotions, and blood was identified with life itself. Yet Protestants too speak about "the blood of the Lamb," celebrated with such hymns as "There is a Fountain Filled with Blood"—creating in us "a heart that always feels thy blood, so freely shed for me." This is a graphic way for naming the love of Jesus as identical with the gift of his life so that we "may have life, and have it abundantly" (John 10:10 RSV).

It is no huge jump, then, to understand why the symbol for Valentine's Day is the heart. To send a card saying "I give you my heart" has nothing to do with a promised transplant, but is a vow of total love. The prophet Hosea has much to teach us about the heart as a loving exchange. God, desperate for us to experience his incredible love for us, chose Hosea to experience and express for all of us what it feels like for God to love so deeply and then have it spurned. He has Hosea marry a prostitute named Gomer, with whom he falls in love. But then, in spite of her professed love for him, she keeps sneaking down the back stairs after dark. Hosea is heartbroken. Now, says God, you are feeling what it is like for me to have wedded my people Israel, only to have her break our marriage vows over and over again.

Scripture is a story of this intensifying divine grief, until it becomes overwhelming in the event called Jesus. In effect, on the cross we behold God dying of a broken heart. Abandoned, spit upon, ridiculed, rejected by his own disciples, and jeered at by crowds that only a week before had professed with jubilation their commitment to him. We are that lying Peter experiencing a knowing glance by Jesus; we are that soldier with a spear in one hand and Christ's blood on the other. In fact, the defining theme of Scripture is God's tragic love affair with us, back stairs and all.

After having been caught in an affair, a friend of mine sobbed in despair, "How can God possibly forgive me?" "Given God's ongoing heartbreak," I replied, "how can he not?" Valentine's Day and Feast of the Most Sacred Heart of Jesus belong together. And as schmaltzy as it might sound, Jesus is God's handwritten message: "Will you be my Valentine?"

79. MARCHING WITH JESUS

Approximately thirty-two weeks out of each year is designated as "Ordinary Time." Yet the church seems to have a hard time letting us live it in any "ordinary" way. Through the centuries it kept inserting special observances—commemorating the Trinity and transfiguration, recollecting saints of all shapes and sizes. One could easily get the impression that we Christians love to party—or at least to celebrate. During the Middle Ages one of these special festivals, called *Corpus Christi* ("Body of Christ"), became so exuberant that it overflowed out onto the village streets. When celebrated in all its fullness, Protestants might not know what to make of it. A consecrated host from the Eucharist was placed in a gold container with a glass front (called a "monstrance," meaning "to show"). Then with a golden canopy carried over it, the priests, town officials, and dignitaries marched with "Jesus" through the city streets, pausing at special places to bless that spot and the faithful who were lining the route.

II. LIVING THE SEASONS

However one might respond to such drama, there is something to be said for witnessing publicly that our God is not distant, remote, disengaged, or unknowable. On the contrary, God is in our midst, madly in love with all of his creation, with us, and intensely interested in all that we do. Each human being is irreducible, one of a kind, irreproducible, with the Holy Spirit establishing a unique spiritual residency within each Christian. We are the fulfillment of Christ's promise to be an ongoing incarnate presence everywhere, luring each portion of life into fullness. Early on, the church dramatized this intimate presence by using a kitchen table as altar, gathering around it with freshly baked bread and home-fermented wine, celebrating the God who eats and drinks with us in all our common day ordinariness (Rev 3:20 RSV).

Therefore it may not be too strange after all if we march with this God who talks, dines, and lives with us, right out into the streets, through the markets, under the bridges, by the gas station, into the jail, through city hall, and around the tables in the soup kitchen. What a fine public witness that would be of the God who goes everywhere—with us in feeding the hungry, healing the sick, befriending the lonely, insisting on justice for all, and establishing peace. When Jesus declared that "the poor you will have with you always," he was promising that as Emmanuel ("God with us") he would be with us always in that task—because "as you do it to one of the least of these who are members of my family, you do it to me"—and with me (Matt 25:40 RSV). Whatever symbolism for this a church might chose, let us take Jesus out from our churches, publicly making our own pilgrimage a "scavenger hunt" for the world—providing hints of Christ in all his various disguises, everywhere and always.

80. MEMORIAL DAY AS ONCE IT WAS

While Memorial Day for most persons is simply a day off to signal the beginning of summer, its origin is profound. After the Civil War, the mother of a dead Confederate soldier honored her son by putting flowers on the graves of Union soldiers as well—inviting others to remember both sides of that tragic conflict, helping to bring hostility of heart to an end.

Some years ago I spent a sabbatical in Alsace-Lorraine. Both France and Germany had long laid claim to this adjoining territory, producing so many violent clashes that since 1900 the inhabitants there had been forced to change citizenship six times. During World War II, the Germans "freed" the residents by making them German citizens, drafting their youth into the army. When the allies, in turn, "freed" them by making them French citizens, the remaining youth were drafted into the opposing army. The result was a horrendous bloodshed of brothers against brothers. When the war was finally over, citizens of the tiny village of Obernai constructed a large cross on their hill. On its base were engraved these words: "For our children, who fought each other, and died alone—but not forgotten. God, never again."

A year later, I went with my cousin to the small cemetery overlooking the Appalachian town of my birth. She and I were the only persons left to continue the family's traditional Memorial Day pilgrimage to plant flowers on the graves of our relatives. The cemetery is traditionally Protestant, with a small section grudgingly marked off for Catholics. When we finished our task, we reminisced as we wandered among the gravestones, finding ourselves in the Catholic section where we had not been before. Along the far fence were some long neglected graves. After pulling the weeds, we looked strangely at each other. Why not? Off we went to buy more geraniums. Such a diminutive act, and yet, as I later learned, it was a hint of what Memorial Day is to be about.

81. MEMORIAL DAY AND CEMETERY REMEMBRANCE

I am beginning to see more frequently in our local newspaper obituaries something that a decade ago would hardly ever have happen. The death of the person is announced, but there is to be no wake or funeral. This seems to reflect our culture in which many folks are feeling so insignificant during their lives that they would feel it hypocritical to be liturgically remembered when they die.

How sadly contrasting this is to my experience at the monastery one December afternoon. It had snowed all day, leaving twelve inches of the white stuff, a searing wind, and temperatures near zero. Reading comfortably in my cell, I glanced out the window. There was a dark figure in the cemetery—just standing, unmoved, unmoving. After a minute or so, I became concerned, reaching for my coat. Then the figure moved, trudging on to the next grave. With such a pained, aged shuffle that could only be Br. Christopher. I was waiting when he reentered, handing him a hot chocolate. He shared his ministry of praying daily at the grave of each monk, by name, no matter what the weather—"helping God to remember." This was where his special friends were resting. And then, several years later, Br. Christopher joined them—and it is my turn to do what he had taught me that afternoon.

All of this recalls the first Memorial Day when as a small boy my father took me with him as he planted flowers on the graves of relatives. I became concerned about a grave over by the fence, covered with weeds. A worn stone called her "Annie." I pulled as many weeds as I could, and transplanted a dandelion. To this day, I offer a special prayer for those who believe that no one cares whether they live or die—not even God.

82. FATHER'S DAY AND GOOD OLD DAD

Mother's Day is a firmly entrenched custom in the United States, with a recent poll indicating that on that day 82 percent of all mothers are gifted by their dutiful offspring. Mom and apple pie—it's the thing to do. But when we come to Father's Day, things get sticky. More than 50 percent of fathers do not receive as much as a card, while those that are sent are usually humorous, void of sentiment. It may be indicative that while Catholic calendars award thirteen yearly feast days to Mary, only two are named for Joseph—and even so, one is as a "worker" and the other as "the husband of Mary."

Apparently we do not quite know what to do with our fathers. Often in the counseling I do, it is "good old dad" who emerges as a core problem. A typical comment is, "I know he must have loved me, *but* . . . ." No, that person doesn't know, and that is the issue. Deep in each of us is the need to be told. And those of us left to guess are damaged merchandise. Every one of my male friends who saw *Field of Dreams* cried. Maybe it's a man thing—but maybe not. My father was even a semi-professional baseball player, yet never once did he play ball with me. Instead, I would throw a rubber ball at a chalk-drawn square on the garage door—playing pitch by myself. I watched the movie more than once. Each time I sobbed when the dead father came back to ask his son, "Hey kid, do you want to play catch?" Yes, yes I do! But he never asked.

It is no surprise, then, that many folks have problems with God understood as "Father." Even as adults, that name continues to evoke in many of us images of a deity who is aloof, or stern, or demanding, or evidencing a speedy temper—inducing a Christianity of dutiful effort to please a deity who can't be pleased, obey a God for whom one can never seem to do enough, and follow a rule-giver by whom we are told we never seem to get it right. For better or worse, for all of us, early experiences shape our faith.

I find it helpful to rename some of Jesus' parables so that they can better touch my own life situation. Thus instead identifying the theme as "The Prodigal Son Who Returns Home," I experience it as "The Loving Father Who Runs out to Embrace His Son." Was Joseph an introvert carpenter who kept reprimanding his boy for touching his tools? Probably not, for one of the most radical aspects of Jesus' teaching is his favorite name for God. It is "abba," which we translate as "father" but its real meaning is closer to "daddy." I know of no one before Jesus who dared to relate to the Almighty Creator of Heaven and Earth in such an intimate way. This may relate to the fact that Jesus seems to have lost his foster father at an early age. God increasingly became for him the dad for whom he yearned. Applied to myself as a prodigal son, I have no need for "the best robe" or a "fatted calf." All I need is a God who asks me, "Hey kid, do you want to play catch?"

83. INDEPENDENCE DAY AND CHRISTIAN PATRIOTISM

The church continues to have difficulty figuring out what to do with the First Amendment's separation of church and state. It could imply that our Christianity is to be restricted to personal, home, and church matters, walled off so as to render public issues out of bounds as purely "secular" matters. Yet this seems not to have been the intent of the First Amendment, for its stated purpose is twofold: to guarantee that no *particular* religion will be awarded official or privileged status; and to protect the "free exercise" of religion. In the case of Christianity, "exercising" involves functioning in society as a prophetic leaven, for otherwise we lose a vital part of our reason for being. Thus while this rightly means that churches are not to impose their doctrines or religious practices on others, we are guaranteed our right to help determine a nation's moral rudder. Even more, since Christianity is committed to a God who enfolds all nations in a loving embrace, the church must transcend the narrow self-interests of any particular nation, called to be a light to the whole earth and salt for flavoring what it means for all persons to be human.

The Old Testament prophets can serve as models, for they functioned as spiritual directors for their nation in general and for their political leaders in particular—providing a feedback mirror, whether invited or welcomed. Where their prophetic judgment came heaviest regarded the neglect and violation of the rights of the poor, widows, orphans, and aliens. Their bottom-line insistence was that destruction awaits any nation in which justice and peace do not embrace and kiss.

Relatedly, the constitutional foundation for the United States declares that all persons "are created equal, that they are endowed by their Creator with certain inalienable rights, that among these are Life, Liberty, and the pursuit of Happiness." The very reason for our government is an ongoing vigilance to "secure these rights." Our rootedness in being "one nation under God" means that all persons are created for equality, in turn having a mutual responsibility to work for the "general Welfare," guaranteeing to each the right to "secure the Blessings of Liberty." The working assumption here is that there is to be a level playing field on which each person receives sufficient opportunities for attaining the means of happiness. These are not rights to be earned but guarantees given each person as a birthright. If we lose this foundation, Lincoln declared, our country will perish from the face of this earth.

What follows is that the indispensable public role for the church is misdirected by insisting on compulsory prayer in public schools or in displaying the Ten Commandments in public places. Our Christian responsibility is to insist upon perpetuating the very foundation of this nation—that every human life is sacred, formed in the likeness of God. When this underpinning becomes eroded, when it becomes functionally disregarded, that is when we have our present crisis—in which this "sweet land of liberty" becomes a competitive jungle in which both corporations and individuals feel license to do to others whatever they can get away with. Without an accountable commitment to the "common good," freedom is another name for greed run wild.

Unfortunately, some churches that do become socially active often become blinkered by an obsession with one particular issue, even fighting other Christians with animosity. Instead, we need to recognize that each concern needs to be seen as one part within the total interlinking of our public task. The Christian responsibility is to see that the inalienable dignity of each person is translated into concrete means for its fulfillment, from life's beginning to its end.

Furthermore, Christianity brings to the task a realism about the sinfulness of our human condition, clarity about how the social network into which a person is born is a significant determiner of self-realization. "Originating sin" is an apt name for it. Thus while churches are doing fairly well in helping to alleviate the symptoms of an unjust system, we must do better in confronting the causes. This entails challenging any social system operating on naked self-interest, insisting on structural accountability sufficient to guarantee respect for the "common good." The church's prophetic responsibility is to maintain a creative tension between freedom "from" and freedom "for," tempering rights with duties, liberty with responsibility. And such diligence is unending. The odds are that for every ten attempts at justice we will be fortunate to have one victory, and that victory will likely need to be re-fought in the near future.

While fear has deeply assaulted our society since 9/11, the real enemy is more within this nation than outside it. In the first place, the United States was created as an experiment worth trying. It is still being tested, and the evolving that our nation is presently undergoing is determining whether or not our experiment has within itself the seeds of its own demise. Second, we are being tested as to whether or not the means that we are using to defend our way of life may be undoing that which makes it worth preserving.

So on this Independence Day, let us be clear that we are Christians who happen to be Americans, not Americans who happen to be Christians. Let us re-filter our patriotism by re-singing the songs of our heritage. A good start might be the *Battle Hymn of the Republic*: "As Christ died to make [people] holy let us die to make them free." And from *America*: "Our Fathers' God to thee, Author of liberty, to thee we sing . . . great God our King." And from *America the Beautiful*: "God shed his grace on thee and crown thy good with brotherhood, from sea to shining sea." And let us draw our benediction from the second verse of the *Star Spangled Banner*: "Praise the Power that has made and preserved us a nation." Christian patriotism never vows "my country right or wrong," but "my country to make right by confessing what is wrong."

84. INDEPENDENCE DAY FOR ALL

I was the most patriotic boy in our neighborhood. I saved my allowance for buying penny American flags to decorate our 1936 Plymouth every Fourth of July—as if it was to be the lead car in a parade. Scouting became my life, and I enthusiastically pledged to "do my duty to God and Country." In our backyard I installed an American flag on a long rusty pipe salvaged for a quarter from the junkyard. Our neighbors were barely amused by my

II. LIVING THE SEASONS

playing "reveille" and "taps" beneath it each morning and evening. I was the first scout in my county to earn the "God and Country" award. Over my bed was a poster of the Statue of Liberty with its words: "Give me your tired, your poor, your huddled masses yearning to breathe free . . . ." I had a nightmare once of being born in a country other than the United States.

Things began changing the evening my black friend was refused membership in our church-sponsored scout troop. Then there was the time in college when I brought my African American college roommate home on spring vacation. I was unprepared for the behavior of my shocked parents. After discrete whispers about "how long" he would be staying, mother concluded that he should use the back door "out of respect for the neighbors." As my seminary teaching became increasingly oriented toward social justice and poverty ministries, conscience led me and my family to move from suburbia into the core city—into the environment where the police, stores, schools, and banks were no longer oriented toward "winners." The poster in my faculty office had a quote from Martin Luther King Jr.: "A nation that continues year after year to spend more money on defense than on programs of social justice is approaching spiritual death." A week before Dr. King was assassinated on the balcony of the Lorraine Motel in Memphis, that motel had placed this ad in a Memphis newspaper: "Vacation here—the one place where negroes won't be hassled or humiliated."

On this present Independence Day, I feel particularly sad that we are building hundreds of miles of walls and electric fences with overhead drones along our southern border—to "solve our immigrant problem." Indelible remain the final words on the poster above my boyhood bed, the part about "the wretched refuse of your teeming shore; send these the homeless tempest-tossed to me; I lift my lamp beside the golden door."

I have not lost my patriotism but it has expanded, best conveyed in a hymn called *This is My Song*. The words begin by celebrating the incredible beauty of this nation which is "my home, the country where my heart is." Then it affirms that there are other lands that have sunlight and clover and skies "as blue as mine." Finally we sing our prayer to the "God of all the nations" in a "song of peace" that embraces other persons in other lands who have "hopes and dreams as true and high as mine."

How fine if this Independence Day evening we Christians set off our fireworks in salute to an international patriotism, loving our nation as pledge to the "Lord of all earth's kingdoms" that our deepest citizenship is to an inclusive kingdom of another kind.

85. TRANSFIGURATION AS PROMISE

It is ironic that the Feast of the Transfiguration is celebrated on the same day as the dropping of the atomic bomb on Hiroshima (August 6). This city, known for the large number of Christians who lived there, underwent on that day in 1945 an extermination of over 100,000 persons, with deaths of countless more continuing to this day. The word "transfigure" means "to change appearance." On the height above Hiroshima, a cloud brought a demonic change of appearance to the innocent people in the unsuspecting city below. In contrast, on the height called Transfiguration, a cloud brought divine promise of hope for the suffering humanity in the valley below. With the Mount of Transfiguration two other mountains were symbolically linked. There Jesus was seen with Moses who on Mount Sinai established Israel's *priestly* tradition, and with Elijah who on Mount Carmel established the *prophetic* tradition. What we are experiencing is that these two foundation dimensions of Israel's life are converging in Christ as the instituting of the kingdom of God. "I have not come to abolish the law and the prophets but to fulfill them." Christ is Priest, Prophet, and now King—in the expansive covenant promise of a transfigured heaven and earth (Mark 9:1f RSV).

Long ago God made clear the implications, and it was Hiroshima that underscored them indelibly with radiation: "I have set before you life and death, blessing and curse; therefore choose life, that you and your descendants may live" (Deut 30:19 RSV). An either/or choice it is—risking a transfiguring nightmare with the nuclear obliteration of our planet, or the Christian dream of a transfigured creation in which Christ shall dab away the world's tears with his resurrection napkin. That is indeed the choice. Transfiguration anticipates resurrection, and resurrection promises transfiguration—gift-wrapped together. A hymn asks God to "help us live as we believe." To believe in the transfiguration is to live "as if" the kingdom is already here—called to transfigure with compassionate love a world that is swaying on the edge of self-consuming anger. Last week a friend said this of her pastor: "When he distributes communion, he glows." What better witness that the Eucharist is our Feast of the Transfiguration.

86. LABOR DAY AND BEYOND

This last holiday of the summer isn't what it used to be. In part I blame the schools. As a boy, Labor Day's significance was as the final day of freedom.

II. LIVING THE SEASONS

My mother amazed me in how she knew that on the very next day after this holiday the water would suddenly be too cold to permit swimming. But it hardly mattered since the day after Labor Day began the imprisonment called school. I knew a few kids who actually liked school, but I kept away from them, praying for their sanity. But today Labor Day has been robbed of its liturgical finality, for school boards have dared to move school openings up into August!

Labor Day was always embraced by a picnic with relatives. It hardly mattered that Uncle Glenn told the same jokes; that there would be a decided discrepancy about what qualified as a well-done hamburger; that someone would surely forget an essential such as ketchup or relish; that the perennial war with ants would be a standoff; and that the only serious argument would be over the relative merits of this year's watermelon over last.

But the part I cherished most was sitting together around a fire as the evening mellowed out with fireflies, listening as the adults reminisced about times and persons that they dared not to forget, as if needing assurance that the past would remain alive in us kids. Significantly, what was remembered were rarely things like accomplishments or awards or degrees—none of the stuff over which the persons probably labored intensely. The fond memories were about the little things, often causing uproars of appreciative laughter. There were stories of when Harvey tripped and fell into Lizzie's lap, and the rest was marriage; or the ever expanding size of the fish supposedly caught during the men's trip to Canada. We remembered the mistakes and misfortunes and disappointments too, but they were made smile-able in the redemptive haze of memory. This was the evening for reaffirming who we were through those who once had been, sufficient to keep our identity warm through the winters of our discontent. A person's death was the entrance initiation into the family folklore. It really began after the formal funeral liturgy, when over coffee around a kitchen table, often with mischievous eyes, the recalling began of new stories being adopted into the family heritage. I often wonder what symbolic smidgens of my life will get woven into the Labor Day retelling.

Scripture originated in a similar way, as a retelling for remembering—long before anyone thought of writing down the family memoirs. The Bible is all about storytelling, each writer gathering the stories and providing his own touches of redemptive haze. Worship is a bit like those Labor Day evenings, when Israel gathered around campfires on the far side of the Red Sea—to tell the story lest it be forgotten. "We have heard with our ears, O

God, our ancestors have told us . . ." (Ps 44:1 NRSV). Likewise the church gathers around a table to eat bread and drink wine while remembering events and singing about the characters. Worship is a "sacred picnic" for savored re-remembering. The sign of being adopted into the body of Christ is the ability to tell these sacred stories as one's own, fleshing them out with one's own life memories—rehearsing together who we were as prelude to the ongoing story of what together we are to become.

An African American tradition likens heaven to a fish fry reunion picnic. All the folks will be there, and with tears and laughter we will participate in retelling the stories of how they got here. And amidst the limitless catfish, God will have the best stories to tell—about each of us. I feel OK about this, because Jesus is God's kindly promise not to blemish the tales, but to embellish them with his own redemptive haze.

87. HALLOWEEN OR THE GOBLINS WILL GET YOU

Halloween, interestingly, has become second only to Christmas as the leading commercial holiday in this country. It has an interesting history. The name that Christians give to the evening before All Saints' Day is "All Hallows' Eve." "Hallow," meaning "holy," refers to the saints, but our society has secularized this time by calling it "Hallow-een." The original meaning is still preserved in Mexico as "The Day of the Dead," with festivities in cemeteries where families picnic happily among the graves of their ancestors, inviting the spirits of the deceased to participate in this celebration of death in life as life through death.

Halloween is intended to be the church's invitation to the "communion of saints," both the living and the dead, to participate in an All Saints' homecoming (November 1), continuing the next day as All Souls' Day in thankful remembrance of all "the faithful departed." But the secularization of this tradition has tended to make Halloween the very opposite. Now it reflects a *fear* of the dead, concocting a scary lot of ghosts, goblins, and skeletons, rising from graves to haunt and scare people. The thought of our dead returning to us has become fearsome. How else are we to understand Halloween's contemporary escalation into a frightening observance, successfully complete with commercially concocted "haunted houses," horror movies, and TV vampire episodes—guaranteeing abundant adrenalin flow? Although supposedly our secular society has long ago given up its belief in such things as ghosts and spirits, I still doubt that many folk would walk through a graveyard at midnight without feeling at least a bit squeamish. In fact, a realtor told me that houses located near cemeteries have a decidedly lower resale value.

Perhaps this phenomenon of Halloween is testifying that in our mechanized, computerized, scientific ethos there remains an outer edge of yearning for something more, to be teased by the inexplicable, faced down by the inscrutable, even frightened into feeling something akin to what our ancestors called "the fear of God." Or looking at the consumer side of contemporary Halloween, for which millions of dollars are spent for costumes, might it be that in the plodding boredom of our daily world, we have so lost our sense of play that we are attracted by any excuse for acting up? Or can it be that in a society in which persons are reduced to numbers, we hunger to be unique, to be different, to pose as someone else, if only through an imitation lasting the length of a masquerade party. Or is it that in our culture saturated by materialism, the Holy Spirit is not letting us squeeze totally dry the strange lure of mystery? At any rate, on this strange day called Halloween, as we contemplate what countenance to carve on the face of our pumpkin, let it be an occasion for pondering what all this might really be about.

88. ALL SAINTS', SOULS', AND IMAGINATIVE MEMORY

All Saints' Day is a time for remembering the official saints. It is followed by All Souls' Day, set aside to celebrate the unofficial ones. There is solid reason for celebrating them together because only God is qualified to distinguish the all-stars. In fact, the marks of "saintliness" are far from constant, depending considerably on the tastes and circumstances of the time in which a "saint" lived. While applauded in their own day, some saints are likely to be seen today as neurotics. Thus what really matters is not so much what they did as to their inner motive for living as they did. In *Murder in the Cathedral*, T. S. Eliot perceptively portrays the primal temptation of St. Thomas Becket in facing his possible martyrdom as doing the right thing for the wrong reason.

In the early church, infants at baptism were given the name of a saint. Some churches still do so by giving adolescents a "confirmation name." In the secular arena, children are often named for a parent or a cherished relative. Such practices testify in their own way that those who have lived before us are part of who we are today. Knowledge of this continuing "incarnation" is expanding through studies about the ongoing power of DNA, language, culture, gender, ethnicity, geography, and tradition. Within the darkened womb we were being formed not only by the lifestyle of our mother, but our groping is mysteriously akin to that of our caved ancestors by torchlight. And our teenage years have a bewitching affinity with the awakening we call the Renaissance.

Thus far from coming naked into this world, we are honed as a composite of all that has gone before, each of us pushed out onto the forward edge of inimitability. Thus in each "now" we are responsible for either tarnishing or redressing the past by how we live our discrete portion of the Holy Spirit's ongoing experiment called history. The philosopher Hegel called each of us a "concrete universal," being who we are because of everything else that exists, as each of our acts ripples back to the edges of everything.

Christian tradition witnesses powerfully to this organic nature of humankind by understanding itself as the *body of Christ*. The church is not simply a human institution but a divine-human reality as the ongoing incarnation of the Christ who was as fully divine as he was fully human. In baptism, Christians are immersed in their separateness into wholeness, raised as new creatures organically connected—analogous, says Paul, of each part of a physical body contributing necessarily to the ongoing functioning of the whole. This new reality embraces not only the living but an interactive memory with the dead, as "so great a cloud of witnesses." The DNA of the church spans space and time, from beginning to end, calling for all of us together to "run with perseverance the race that is set before us, looking to Jesus the pioneer . . ." (Heb 12:1–2 RSV).

Thus during these two "saintly" days of remembrance, let us give thanks for each soul who has ever lived, for better or for worse. Each one of them has had a part in our birthing and, in turn, is gambling on our becoming. The church's commission is to see that none of them have lived in vain—as we preserve the best of what they were able, and redeem the failures whose repentance we must now assume. As their spirits live now in the lively memory of God, so also are they humanly enfleshed in us. The holiness of the saints is strangely at stake in our own short lives, for it is the quality of our living that can counter society's dismissive estimate of them, and us—as naïve, misguided, irrelevant, foolish, dated, and a bit quaint.

II. LIVING THE SEASONS

89. ALL SAINTS' AND LONELINESS

Care centers and nursing homes can be lonely places. The sadness is almost palpable as one walks down the hall trying often in vain to elicit a smile from the forgotten ones lining the walls. Once vibrant, many of them are now part of the forgotten, slobbering "refuse." When those who once cared about them are now absent or dead, abandonment is an unwieldy feeling. Actually this earth can be a very lonely even in the midst of crowds. The memory of my first day in kindergarten still clings to me—when as an only child, my mother left me to be exiled in a clamoring room of thirty diminutive strangers.

One of the most precious of pastoral roles is to offer persons "the body of Christ" at the Eucharist. One by one they come forward. Often our eyes meet—deep, pleading, enduring much. Many are what I call the "walking wounded." The chalice lifted at the altar holds not only the blood of Christ's suffering but the pain of us all—the lame, the blind, the rejected, the sick, the anxious, the unwanted, the lonely, receiving the promise of Christ's hug. The elements held before each person's eyes are a declaration that is intended as a question for the communicant. This bread of the world's brokenness, "Is this the body of Christ, *really*?" This wine of the world's suffering, "Is this the blood of Christ, *really*?" "Amen," meaning "so be it," is the invited answer.

I was not prepared for the power of what happened at my ordination. I was to drop to the floor, arms spread out in the form a cross, face pressed into the floor. Dying to the past, I would be raised in marked newness—as the congregation chanted the names of the saints who were embracing me as witnesses. "St. Paul, pray for us." On and on came the cascade of requested prayers, from Aquinas to Luther, from Wesley to Mother Teresa—thirty-three in all. Someone in the congregation, misunderstanding what was happening, gasped, "Will someone please help that man!" In all truth, I had been helped beyond knowing.

The church is far more than the building on the corner by the gas station, its basement smelling of mildew. It is the body of Christ himself, the one slain from the foundations of the earth for the redemption of the universe. Thus even the tiniest of shabby churches is "surrounded by so great a cloud of witnesses" that it extends from the beginning of time to its end (Heb 12:1 RSV)—sealed with the guarantee that "the powers of death shall not prevail against it" (Matt 16:18 RSV). So identified, may we celebrate All Saints' Day as a powerful affirmation for a world mightily in need. When embraced within the arms of the church as our mother, one can never again be lonely. We belong, adopted, enfolded, in the embrace of eternity.

90. ALL SOULS' DAY AND GOING HOME

St. Paul's last words to the church at Ephesus are a sad but courageous sharing. "None of you will ever see my face again." Yet "I do not count my life of any value to myself, if only I can finish my course and the ministry that I have received from the Lord Jesus has assigned me, to bear witness to the gospel of God's grace" (Acts 20:25,24 NAB). We are reminded of the farewell words of Jesus in John's gospel when he "knew that his hour had come" (John 3:1f RSV).

I was raised in a small depressed town in Appalachia. The houses were propped up on the side of a mountain with the mine shafts yawning on the opposite hill. "Boney piles" of smoking slag snuffed the life out of the trees, as a yellow sulfur creek worked its smelly way down through the valley once green. Yet in the clearer air on the height overlooking the valley was the cemetery, always cleanly maintained. While it was well regarded as the sleeping place for the dead, it served as well as a center for the living. It was where people went for walks on Sunday afternoons. My first date was a hand-in-hand stroll to that cemetery. People picnicked there, using the tombstones as tables. Memorial Day was our Protestant "All Souls' Day," called "Decoration Day" because it was when we planted flowers on the graves. They were always geraniums and bachelor buttons because they were the only ones able to brave the soot, wind, and drought. One could hardly walk among the graves without telling stories, for they were all family, the dead among the living.

Back in the days of my parents, there was never a question about where one would be buried. Folks never moved very far away from that cemetery on the hill. But now, in the transient society in which we all live, most folks no longer have a clear "home" to which their bodies can be returned for burial. Symbolic of this homelessness was the sadness shared during a phone call with a friend who had recently "honored" her mother's request to "just throw my ashes into the ocean." I still feel the pain for a dear colleague whose body after suicide was quickly cremated and his ashes scattered by his wife, robbing me of a "place" that I could visit and ask "why." The chaplain at the local nursing home told me this story. "This old man was dying, so I put my ear close to his lips to hear what he was struggling to say. 'I don't want to die,' he finally got out. 'I don't have anywhere to go.' Then he died."

My five daughters are scattered across the country, wherever their vocations take them, for the time being. We always gather for Christmas, and at one such celebration I asked where each would want to be buried. The conversation immediately floundered. Typical of their generation, none of them had remained long enough in any one place to claim it as "home." Even if each were to choose the different city in which she had been born, there would likely be no friends remaining there to remember. With approving smiles one of them suggested, "How about planting my ashes on top of Mount Sopris, the first mountain we all climbed together?"

There is a burial plot in that Appalachian cemetery waiting for me, next to my parents who are "expecting" me to come home. But as a Family Brother of the Trappist Order, I also have the option of being buried at the monastery. When I had not yet decided, my abbot expressed pastoral concern. "If you were to be buried with your parents, would there be anyone left to pray at your grave? Here with us, you will be fondly remembered daily." Before deciding, I felt the need to return to my birthplace one final time. I tried to imagine a hearse taking my body through the narrow street between the miners' houses, and up the hill. I still have coal dust in my lungs. Maybe if I could believe that a faint sound of Mozart might come through an open window. But looking out from that windblown hill, I knew. You can't go home again.

And there, in the twilight overlooking the town of my birth, I realized how powerful the choice of one's burial location is. It symbolizes what one sees one's life as having been about. Where should it be in order for that symbolic choice to witness with St. Paul that we have done our best to run faithfully the race and finished the course God has given us? An added blessing it would be if a few friends were left to say an occasional "Amen" of support at our grave site. This is why churches used to have a graveyard in their backyard—just to make sure we all remembered where home is.

91. CHRIST THE KING—MAYBE AND ALMOST

Christ the King is the climax of the church year, celebrated on the last Sunday of November as the promised crescendo of history. Easter is its foretaste, and Pentecost is its enablement. At the beginning of time, the morning stars danced with joy as they beheld the earth being created as the theater of God's glory. The center point of this divine-human drama occurs when the Playwright himself appears on stage, Star of the play within the Play. Therein is distilled the plot of history—the dynamic of creation, fall, incarnation, crucifixion, resurrection, and ascension into the kingdom. The Holy Spirit is yearning and luring and thrusting this whole cosmic drama toward a glorious crescendo, one best sensed by participating in the chorus from Handel's Messiah: "And he shall reign forever and ever." Everything in history points toward, evolves with, and participates in this dynamic of God becoming "all in all." In lifting the chalice at Holy Communion we toast this promised coronation banquet that is also the marriage feast of the Lamb with the cosmos as spouse.

When guests come to a friend's house for a special dinner party, they often bring a gift. To Christ's promised banquet, the invitation reads: "You will be gift enough." I prefer this kind of culmination over the folklore finale of pearly gates armed by angelic homeland security police frisking frightened candidates with ominous questions. As we have been exploring in this book, the Christian year begins anew with Advent, and from there we work our way through the Christmas foretaste into a Lenten disciplining in order for us to become ourselves the resurrection gifts worth offering at the celebration of Christ the King.

The brilliant philosopher Ernest Becker discerned something of this in concluding that "the lived truth of creation" is that the most any one of us can seem to do is "to fashion something—an object or ourselves . . . and make an offering of it," dropping it into the mystery. Jesus' version uses the imagery of talents given at birth in hopes that they will be returned at death with increase. Actually, in anticipation of this coronation event, he has entered on his "gift registry" his preferred gifts: food for the hungry, drink for the thirsty, and hospitality for the enemy.

92. IS THIS MESS GOD'S IDEA?

This feast of "Our Lord Jesus Christ King of the Universe" is a fine finale for our church year, providing as it does a hopeful vision for history's culmination in the kingdom of God. And yet what it promises can be a stumbling block to being a Christian. It seems too good to be true. The conditions of today's world seem to defy all such hope. We are fortunate if we have never been shot, imprisoned, tortured, or experienced starvation, for half a billion of the world's population has. We are fortunate if we have food in our refrigerators, clothes to wear, or a roof over our heads, for if we do, we are better off than 75 percent of the world. We are fortunate if we have any money in the bank, for that puts us in the top 8 percent of the world's wealthy. Thus instead of going forward with Palm Sunday joy to celebrate the glorious "coronation promise" of Christ the King, many persons in our world are stuck back at Good Friday crying, "My God, why have you forsaken [us]?"

Why, indeed! The Christian must face head on this question—is this horrendous mess of our world God's doing, is it God's idea, or is it the result of God's indifference? Yet while we Christians must answer "No," how do we know otherwise? *The cross*. The crucified King is the definitive declaration that not only are suffering and death not God's doings, but in being our enemies they are God's foes as well. Instead of God being the determining cause of all that is happening, or being a spectator who simply watches the ugly show, our God is the one who takes sides, struggling with us for life over death in the midst of all life's turmoils. The heart of the gospel is the disclosure through Jesus Christ that God is, in Whitehead's term, our "Fellow-sufferer." God with us.

Therefore since God and we are fighting through this mess together, we can trust the unquenchable hope deep inside us. It is this longing, interestingly, that constitutes the appeal of many of our best musicals. The *West Side Story* dreams that "there is a place for us somewhere." Judy Garland searches for that somewhere "over the rainbow" where skies are actually blue. *The Man from La Mancha* sings of being lured by the "impossible dream." *Carousel* longs for the golden sky at the "end of the storm." *The Sound of Music* bids us climb every mountain, until we "find the dream."

Marx could be right, that the Christian vision is a sentimental and naïve opiate, seducing us the masses into a compensatory toleration for being exploited now. Freud might be right that Christianity is an illusory crutch for those of us unable to face honestly the terror woven into existence. And yet it might just be that this visionary persistence in hope is the enticing of the Holy Spirit, yearning us forward from within, and luring with horizons without. Without vision the people perish, for otherwise we are reduced to living what Shakespeare characterizes as "a tale told by an idiot, full of sound and fury, signifying nothing."

Christian faith is the act of uniting belief with will through vision. Therefore may we defiantly celebrate "Christ the King" today as a crescendo to our church year, when in the face of all evidence to the contrary, we permit ourselves to become intoxicated by the vision of "a new heaven and a new earth" where the God dwelling in our midst shall wipe every tear from our eyes, vanquishing death so that "mourning and crying and pain will be no more." The Christ who is seated on the throne keeps repeating, "See, I am making all things new" (Rev 21:5 NAB). No wonder Augustine marveled that God has "put himself in our debt, not by receiving anything from us but by promising to us so much."

With this vision firmly incarnated in our minds as the underlying "reason for the seasons," we are readied now for the next spiral of our pilgrimage. Next Sunday we begin Advent again, hopefully with a clearer understanding from the meaning we have just lived, as to how to anticipate more fully what is ahead.

www.ingramcontent.com/pod-product-compliance
Lightning Source LLC
Chambersburg PA
CBHW022121160426
43197CB00009B/1114